# MIND MASTERY
# MEDITATIONS

By Valerie V. Hunt

Mailbu Publishing Company
Malibu, California 90265

Publisher's Cataloging in Publication


Hunt, Valerie V.
    Mind mastery meditations / by Valerie V. Hunt - 1st ed.
    p.cm.
    Includes index.
    ISBN 0-9643988-2-6

    1.Meditation--Handbooks, manuals, etc.    I. Title.
BL627.H86 1997                158'.12
                        QBI96-40681




Published by:
Malibu Publishing Co.
P.O. Box 4234
Malibu, CA 90265

(310) 457-4694 - FAX (310) 457-2717


**Printed in the United States of America**

# Dedication

*This book is dedicated to those persons whose minds find new thoughts and great wonders to explore*

# Index

# Chapter I
# INTRODUCTION TO
# MIND MASTERY MEDITATIONS

*M*ind Mastery Meditations are the practical "how you do it" instructions following the information in my recent popular book, *Infinite Mind: Science of the Human Vibrations of Consciousness.*

*Mind Mastery Meditations* are very different from other meditation approaches. Our goals are not simply to give you emotional peace and relaxation. We do not follow ancient beliefs, sacred philosophies or shamanistic rituals. This book is written by popular demand for you who have evaded meditation because it seemed to stress beautiful, unreal symbolic experiences that had no permanent meaning in your life. It is written for you who tried meditation and got nowhere. This book is for you who stopped meditation because it was not sufficiently profitable for the time expended. And this book is written also for you experienced mediators who realize that you are caught up in a consciousness block that your current techniques do not handle.

*Mind Mastery Meditations* give you skills to evolve toward Mastery. The exercises are as literal as the title --- you take control not by repression but by insight and change which frees the mind for its great potential. The mind is no longer a slave to its unconscious urges but is constantly aware of its interaction with external fields of information. Here one can select experiences and respond on a more successful consciousness level.

This book focuses on the mind not on the brain; specifically, it deals with the mind as a function of the mind-field not of the brain tissue *(Infinite Mind, Chapter V, The Mind Field Residence of the Consciousness and the Soul)*. We have discovered that the mind-field holds memory of the souls' experiences from prior lifehoods as well as the unconscious experiences of the "self" in this lifehood. These are residues that influence and often totally direct behaviors that are beyond the domain of brain memories. Because these are not always easy to recall "will power" can be used to control them. Yet, "will power" can never eliminate their influence.

The word "mastery" is connected to the concept of a "master" in the spiritual tradition. But it refers to you as master --- not to some learned one who knows all. Mind Mastery implies both power and wisdom connoting mastery over the external world and the drives and predilections of the inner self; being in control of one's destiny but at the same time realizing the oneness of everything, Mind Mastery does not require the ego to be dampened but rather extends selfhood into the divine level which removes self-imposed restrictions.

Our goals are to open closed recesses of the mind, to access hidden agendas, to eliminate restricting thoughts and to reorder confused emotions. This approach is very different from brain training or biofeedback. The objectives are not the linear, logical solutions of everyday problems. We already know that problems are never solved on the conscious level that we think created the problems. Mind Mastery Meditations allow you to redefine stubborn problems by viewing them at a higher level of wisdom where self-protective emotions don't cloud the issues or elicit the reflexive behaviors from the brain level. Mind Mastery Meditations start with consciousness expansion where you learn what is going on in your "stream of consciousness." If from this discussion you are now motivated to pursue these meditations, take a moment to answer the following questions:

1. Do you believe that you possess far greater capacities than your present accomplishments reflect? Haven't you put out the effort or don't you know how?

2. Do you feel that your mind has its "brakes" on --- that you are stuck so that expending energy only wears out your patience and your body?

3. Do you want to and do you have the ego strength to change old unsuccessful thoughts? And are you willing to look at your most cherished beliefs as a possible source of your blocks?

4. Are you willing to experience and acknowledge your emotional defenses and with deeper understanding to release these? As you open your mind field you will find unrecognized beliefs and experiences that powerfully influence your daily life.

As stated in the Mayan Calendar we are passing from the "Age of Man" to the "Age of Gods," a millennium where we can see, acknowledge and free the beauty of our souls. As we change our awareness we can change the social world with a new and glorious focus upon man's spiritual nature. Our own individual souls, our highest selves, are telling us that mankind has far greater potentials and spiritual powers than we have ever known. Are you eager to be about this work for yourself or are you hesitant?

# ❧ HUMAN CONSCIOUSNESS ☙

2

In this book consciousness is restricted to a human condition. Consciousness is an awareness or a focus on some sensory or mental data that is then recorded in the brain and mind. But awareness is not absolute or always finely pointed. There is always the relativity of awareness; sometimes it is expanded, sometimes truncated. The relativity is determined by the stimulus and the readiness of the brain or mind to pinpoint a focus or to sidetrack information. For example, we know that incoming sensory information is routed throughout a neurological switching station in the brain stem where each individual has programmed what is important in his personal life. He becomes hyper alert to some information and casual with other information.

In this book we envision consciousness on a continuum from subconscious to intellectual cognitive consciousness and to super consciousness. Any level can blend in or out with another level. Because consciousness is awareness and awareness occurs on numerous levels there is no such thing as unconscious behavior. There is non-cortical behavior but as long as life exists there is always awareness of the level of consciousness that exists at the time.

How do we know these things? We scientists who have redefined the mind have discovered vibratory frequency patterns that coexist with patterns of consciousness. Here the mind is found to exist in the field rather than in the denser tissue of the brain. It exists in organized energy containing information from the soul's experience in this and other lifehoods. The field permeates all tissue and radiates around the body. We have simply called it the aura. From such new ideas we can start directly under-standing consciousness.

# ❧ The Human Energy Field & Consciousness ☙

*T*hat the human energy field contains the highest level of the human mind was documented in my Bioenergy Research Laboratory at U.C.L.A. Briefly this is what we discovered:

1. The atomic electrical energy of cells becomes the auric field.

2. The field is both inside and outside of the body where it colors all sensory information that must pass through the field and skin before it gets to the sensory nerve endings.

3. Because the field has a corona on the outside of the body it is in direct contact with all the energies of the environment, living, mineral and celestial. This is the primary way humans interact with the world.

4. The human field is a dynamic ever-changing series of patterns of frequencies that oscillate up to one million cycles per second making it the fastest and most elaborate of the body's electrical systems.

5. Each person has a unique signature pattern of frequencies, his base reference, to which he returns when his field is not stimulated. This is a base reference from which his field responds to other fields.

6. The mind-field is the highest level of memory, containing information about the physical body, thoughts, feeling states and past and present life experiences, particularly if memory is of profound experiences.

7. Emotions connected with higher states of consciousness organize the mind-field and make it susceptible to new and threatening situations. This level of emotion is the deepest motivation of behavior.

*3*

Because our energy field is our primary information gathering source we should not wrap ourselves in "white light" to protect ourselves because this barricades out all the important information that we need. The meditations which follow will help you to open the deeper recessesof your mind which have been closed to conscious awareness.

A field which is flexible and strong with a wide range of frequencies is a stable signature, an ideal resting ground which is complex and well-organized but not chaotic. This is a comfortable field which gives satisfaction, allows exciting discoveries and makes possible exuberant health.

These mind-field concepts lead us directly to the dynamic continuum of consciousness which we call the "stream of consciousness." The stream of conscious awareness is ever shifting. Sometimes awareness is directed to material things, sometimes to mystical and spiritual things and sometimes to survival. The focus of consciousness may move rapidly through all levels simultaneously. Cognitive memory seems to lag behind when memory areas of the brain are stimulated. But consciousness is instant when the memory stored in the mind-field is stimulated.

# ❧ How To Meditate ☙

*M*ind Mastery Meditation, with an internal focus on the stream of consciousness is the best way to broaden the narrow consciousness of most people. Consciousness must include the gross sensory information, nervous system and brain functions incorporated with the subtle information of the mind. The entire field must grow in coherency flowing freely between mind and brain.  As one's everyday stream of consciousness rolls along one needs skills to survey what is going on, one's dreams and daydreams.  The best way to recover this information is through visual imagery.

We know that all information (either sensory or subtle) which drives one's stream of consciousness must first penetrate the surrounding mind-field.  Perceptual research shows that all information is integrated through visual imagery.  Likewise, stimulation of visual imagery brings forth the clearest memory.  However, even with visual imagery we tend to block out parts that are too emotional or we get stuck with only parts of the information such as sound, color or motion.

## ❦ How to Start Meditating: ❧

Locate and christen a place in your home where you will practice Mind Mastery Meditations.  Ideally set aside one room or a part of a room for that purpose.  If possible select a spot away from where you cook, eat, entertain, sleep or watch television to eliminate your preprogramming of the space.  You want no distractions while you discover the non-ordinary mystical levels of your consciousness.  Tell the family that when you are here meditating you are not available.  Also, request that they behave quietly.  Go there daily, at a programmed time if possible to look inside your mind.  Meditation when you find time never works --- you rarely find the time.  Also plan for enough time to swing out of clock time into past and future time where you dream and reverie.  This is all preparation for your deeper meditation.  You may use color, lights or sounds to establish a peaceful mood or to block out sounds but don't rely on these to take you to places you are unwilling to go without them.

Now try to give up your intense "will" to make it happen and your ego needs to be in charge.  And while you are eliminating such personality controls file your rational brain in the hall of in another room.  If it is too demanding tether it outside.  Those are the ways that you try to solve ordinary problems.  Now you are seeking new skills by opening your mind to all its glories, its inconsistencies and its errors of judgment.  Generally, such consciousness clearing doesn't happen during the first meditations.  But it will if you give it time.

Keep uppermost in your thoughts that you have chosen to start Mind Mastery.  Know that your mind has all the answers to why you are as you are.  It has answers to your soul's needs, your unique capacities and your self-designed destiny.  Yes, no one knows exactly how to do this but you will find guidance from a higher source.  A bit of impatience helps but too much discourages you by keeping your meditation on the material level, not where Mind Mastery occurs.  Eventually you can find the greatest excitement balanced by the most profound tranquillity.  But dramatic happenings rarely occur immediately.  Be aware of how long is has taken you to build up barriers and to settle into where you are.

Your job is to learn to access your profound teacher.  At first you may contact "guides" to help you over the insecurities that arise as you seek new information from your higher self.  Guides are comforting for a while but I urge you soon to realize that the guides did not choose you; you chose them based upon your level of awareness and needs.  Start out by asking questions about the answers "you get from them."  Ask them what this information means to you.  If you don't like or understand "their" teachings challenge them so that you can clear up your thoughts.  If information is helpful embrace it as yours because that is where it came from.  Soon I hope you will try to reach that space without your guide.  Give him or her a vacation.  And when

4

you do you will begin to feel your power, that you are in charge. Thank them and bid them adieu. Remember it is weakening to give away your power to some being or guide or to constantly use psychic readers to contact your upper consciousness. Yes, psychic readers can read your thoughts but they also filter these through their minds with what they think is significant. They encourage child-like dependency. Mind Mastery Meditations help you grow up consciously. Mind Mastery comes with your commitment, your insights and your growing awareness. Some of you will still feel weak with a nagging "I don't know how; someone must teach me" attitude. If you feel you can't meditate because you haven't been successful before, recognize that this is simply a defense. Be annoyed at this defense and whenever it comes up be aware and let it go. Ask yourself what you will feel like not to have these doubts. Don't try to "tear them out." That won't work because you will build back that defense or others just as quickly as you consciously eliminate some. Defenses go permanately only when you no longer need or want a false protection from understanding the hidden recesses of your own mind.

## How to Use This Book

After reading this chapter, rapidly survey the remaining chapters for an overview before you begin chapter II, _Activating the Physical._ The first six chapters require that you reach inward into self to expand your consciousness and free your mind. With practice, your consciousness should be quite fluid and your Mind Mastery skills more developed. During meditation on Chapter VII, _Transferring Thought_, you will refocus your awareness outward into the social world to understand and communicate thought through vibrations. In the last chapter, _Sensing the Biocosmic Confluence_, you are asked to focus on the physical world and the outer worlds with the electromagnetic mileau which supports you and the wide ranging vibrations which activate you. You will learn to expand your awareness still further out to sense the constant communications between your biological field and those of the universe. So you will begin to sense how your electromagnetic transactions change us and the cosmos.

5

With the following Mind Mastery Meditations we are primarily concerned with the stream of consciousness of the mind, its wholeness as we become aware of its dynamic qualities on all levels. This means that we extend our stream of consciousness to increase our capacity to integrate all parts of the extended whole where we can select the most important information to solve problems and enliven our lives. This is an enormous task, for it demands the skill to know the most profound information about self -- to change what is unacceptable and to learn to effectively transact with the world.

# Chapter 2
#  ACTIVATING THE PHYSICAL

*T*his chapter will give you the skills to activate your physical energy field. Each of you has created your personal world based on what you consider important. Most people consider material things very real and thus significant. So it's little wonder that you place a special value on your physical body. Regardless of how well or poorly you treat your body, it is always central to your physical life, a reference point for your behavior and the seat of your ordinary consciousness. When you become ill or experience pain you recognize that some change is necessary, so you seek medical attention and improve your health habits. But these actions only treat the dense body and its malfunctions.

Recent research shows that there is another important treatment that is often not considered. The body has a force or an energy field that operates at a deeper and more basic level than systems, tissues and cells. This is where the disturbances are believed to have occurred first, before they appear in the chemical or physiological systems. In other words, your field is sick before your physical body becomes ill.

Experience shows that the healing of injuries or systemic problems is immeasurably hastened when the body's energy field is coherent, flowing smoothly and not blocked. As the dense body is supplied energy from food, so the energy field is activated by the interaction with the electromagnetic energy of the universe through the air one breathes and through the direct interface with the chakras and the acupuncture points. We know from clinical experience that individuals can consciously manipulate and improve the body's energy field with creative imagery. Beginning meditators have particular difficulty quieting their busy minds; however, when they practice imagery focused on their field they learn to meditate more rapidly than if they use esoteric imagery that is unrelated to physical reality. The imagery exercises contained in this chapter are effective in hastening recovery from illness or injury, overcoming fatigue and maintaining physical health. These exercises will also help you to quiet your busy mind before you undertake deeper meditation techniques.

For those of you unacquainted with human electromagnetic fields, let me describe the body's connection. Although the field cannot be perceived easily by the five senses it is readily observable in higher states of consciousness. Focal points in the human field are chakras which are not material substances but are wheel-shaped vortices of energy that were discovered many centuries ago by ancient Eastern philosophers. Although they are more readily felt than seen, chakras have been scientifically validated and found to be in apposition to major neurological plexuses and over primary endocrine glands. Likewise, there are small chakras connected to all joints. Much of the pain from minor joint injuries comes from shock to these chakras. Research has shown a stronger field flowing in and out of the body at these locations --- a communication system between the atomic energy from the cells and molecules with that of the outside environment. Aura readers describe the flow as a vortex like a cyclone or water moving down a funnel. Blockages that occur in the chakra areas stop the smooth flow of energy in and out and up and down the chakras.

# INSTRUCTIONS

## MUSCULAR RELAXATION

*Y*ou will learn to consciously increase the flow and the coherency of the field using conscious imagery. When first learning it's better to lie on your back on a firm surface in a quiet place. Feel your muscle tensions release and rest securely on the firm surface.

❖ First tighten muscles in your feet and legs until you feel the tension quite strongly. Let half of that tension out. Stop and be aware of your feeling of tension. Now let go one half of what remains. Follow with a slow continuous relaxation until your legs rest firmly and the tension in your legs is gone. Pause for a minute feeling the lessened tension.

❖ Now less strongly contract the muscles in your hips and buttocks. Let one half of that tension out. Pause to sense this amount of tension. Now let one half of the remaining tension go. Follow with a slow continuous relaxation. Without pushing downward allow your hips to rest firmly on the supporting surface. Pause again to experience the absence of tension.

❖ Next slightly tighten your arms and shoulders until you feel tension. Let out half of that tension. Hesitate for a few moments to sense the decrease in tension. Now let out one half of the remaining tension. Continue a slow progressive relaxation until your arms rest firmly on the supporting surface. Then let them relax further as though they were dropping downward in water. Hesitate to experience the growing relaxation in your legs, hips and shoulders.

8 ❖ Now lightly tighten the muscles in your neck. These muscles accumulate tension as you attempt to screen out extraneous signals to and from your brain. Visualize your neck as a suspended bridge that sags gently in the middle with the weight carried on your head and shoulders. Allow half of this tension out. Pause to feel the difference. Now allow one half of the remaining tension to go. Follow with a slow continuous relaxation. See if your neck feels like a soft connection between your head and body.

❖ Take a series of full breaths which you let out with a big sigh. This relaxes your diaphragm.

## RELAXATION SCALE

*H*ere is a rapid way to decrease general physical tension in your body.

❖ Imagine that you see a scale of tension from 0 to 100 points: 0 equals a total absence of tension; 100 represents the highest tension the body can tolerate without a nervous collapse; 50 is the level of tension most efficient for ordinary physical and mental work.

❖ Look at your scale; where is your current tension level? What you immediately see is generally correct for the time being. Know that you can systematically lower your tension level at will. Concentrate on lowering the scale and watch it drop progressively 10 or 15 points.

❖ Note your success; hesitate a moment then drop it 10 to 15 more points. Continue lowering your tension scale until you reach 0 or as low as it will go this time.

# ❦ SUGGESTIONS ❧

❀ When you visualize and practice focusing thought on a single point or an idea such as in meditation, regardless of the technique or purpose, the frequency vibrations of the energy field increase and you will experience another level of awareness or consciousness. Simutaneously activity in muscles, nerves and glands decreases.

❀ The energy field vibrations of many beginners may increase rapidly and accumulate in the upper part of the body and even pour out the top of the head. This condition is often called an "out of body" state, because perception is no longer linked to the material body. In fact, usually, memory of an out of body state is limited and often absent. Here, meditation provides an escape rather than providing you with new refined information about yourself, the universe, what has happened or will happen, where you are on your evolutionary path and deep and abiding solutions to your problems. You must be grounded when you soar.

❀ You can progress farther at a later time or another day. This same exercise will effectively lower blood pressures and heart rates. Repeat this imagery scale when you are fatigued, tense or before meditation.

9

# ❧ INSTRUCTIONS ☙

## EARTH GROUNDING

You logical thinkers who rarely daydream are probably already grounded by your strong sense of reality. But for you who tend to daydream with thoughts that fly around, the next exercise is a requisite, before you undertake any further meditation. Grounding yourself means that the energy is flowing in the lower part of your body, anchoring you to the reality of the earth. Meditations that emphasize the upper chakras encourage an ungrounded state that excludes various consciousness levels. Here is a basis grounding image.

❖ Take a full breath as though you were breathing through the bottom of your left foot. Bring the breath up your left leg and across the back of your hips as you inhale.

❖ As you exhale force the breath down the right leg and out the foot deeply into the ground.

❖ Repeat this several times until the circuit is clearly habitual. If you become light headed or dizzy during other meditations, repeat this grounding exercise.

### TETHER LINE

❖ While lying down imagine that you have a strong tight tether line attached to your navel on one end and to a large boulder on the other end. This line holds you firmly to the earth.

10

❖ In between you and the rock there is an automatic reel that you can activate to shorten the tether line and pull you down to earth. Also, you can let out the tether line so that you can drift upward in space and in consciousness while being safely attached to the boulder.

❖ Image bringing yourself close to the rock. Feel the sensation of your feet firmly planted on the earth.

❖ Now allow yourself to drift upward, always aware that the line from your navel is a gentle restraint keeping you from drifting off into space.

❖ Sense how it feels to be grounded yet free to soar.

❖ Experiment with how you feel when firmly grounded and when gently grounded as you go up higher in vibrations.

❖ As you gain skill you will broaden your range to include higher and lower frequencies. This will prepare you to integrate various levels of consciousness.

❖ If you are already strongly grounded spend more time with the tether line exercise. If you tend to be ungrounded be sure to practice the earth grounding exercise.

## INCREASING THE FIELD FLOW

You will need to develop two skills: to activate the movement of your body's energy in and out as well as up and down; and to raise and lower your field's frequencies. To improve the flow in and out and up and down we use the breathing exercises progressing from feet to head.

✤ Starting at the feet, imagine that you have noses at the bottom of your two feet. On each breath inhale energy through your feet up to your abdomen; immediately exhale pushing the energy back down your legs and out your feet. Take normal rather than exaggerated deep breaths and focus your attention on how your legs feel as the energy flows up and down. Do this about ten times or more if you are habitually ungrounded or until you feel you have established a circuit that will continue.

✤ Now focus your awareness on the inside front of your knees, as though your noses were there. As you inhale feel the energy entering your knees and rising into your abdomen. As you exhale, experience the energy flowing downward and out the knees. Repeat ten times or until you are aware that the circuit has become automatic.

✤ Next focus awareness deep in the pelvis, slightly anterior to the rectum (the root chakra). Again pull energy inward with each inhalation and outward on exhalation. It is frequently difficult to feel energy flowing in this area because we experience urination and defecation as outward flows. Here we are working with the energy field which flows in and out.

✤ Now become aware of a location in the lower abdomen where the testes and the ovaries lie. Eastern literature calls this the kundalini. Again breathe in toward the spine and then out from the spine, allowing the energy always to move upward on inhalation and downward and out the lower abdomen on exhalation. These exercises will increase the amount of energy flow and also indirectly will increase circulation of the blood and lymphatic fluid.

✤ Now move your awareness to the solar plexus or your stomach above your waist, which is called the emotional chakra. Because this area of the field is frequently sluggish, you may have difficulty visualizing breath entering easily and smoothly. More than ten breaths may be required to establish a free flow.

✤ Next place your attention on the middle of your body at the heart level. As you breathe through the heart chakra, your chest will fill as the energy moves downward into your abdomen. Strangely, of all the chakras so far visualized, this is the one that is usually most open and free. Ten breaths may be adequate to increase the energy flow here. If you feel that your heart chakra is closed, the sensation generally comes from problems in the emotional chakra not in the heart.

✤ Now focus on the throat chakra in the middle of the "V" above the breast bone. Throat chakra stagnation in adults has been associated with blocked creativity. As you breathe through this chakra be aware of energy going both ways, down on inhalation and coming back up to the throat on exhalation.

✤ Focus your attention on the third eye, located on your forehead just above and between your eyes. Breathe deeply but smoothly through this spot, feeling the air go

11

into the center of your head then downward filling the chest and abdomen without strain. Exhale through the third eye and repeat ten times.

✤ And last, focus on the spot on the top of the head, above your ears. Imagine inhaling air down through this crown chakra into the body and out the crown chakra on exhalation. Repeat ten times. The energies should now be flowing in and out so that your field is expanded by many inches or even feet around your body.

✤ Before you leave this imagery exercise, repeat taking one breath through each chakra into the chest and abdomen. But instead of exhaling back down and out the same chakra, exhale the energy up and out the crown chakra. This way the energy is flowing from each charkra up and out the crown.

✤ If your mind starts wandering during any of these exercises, go back to the knees with a few breaths. This will ground you rapidly.

✤ Now focus on the feeling in your feet, the insides of the knees, the bottom of the pelvis, the kundalini, the emotional chakra, the heart chakra, the throat chakra, the third eye and the crown chakra. Spend a few minutes now settling in, observing and being aware of what your electromagnetic field feels like when it freely flows in and through your body in all directions.

12

# INSTRUCTIONS

## INCREASING ENERGY FREQUENCIES

You should learn to increase your vibrations in all ranges: high, low and in the middle ranges to stabilize the field before attempting deeper meditation. We no longer emphasize just going up in vibrations but rather in filling a wide range of frequencies from low to high with all in between. With health, happiness and successful meditations your range of frequencies expands. With disease and emotional disturbance the range decreases.

To expand your frequency range it is helpful to imagine each chakra spinning clockwise while visualizing a corresponding color. (In the northern hemisphere water flows clockwise down a drain; in the southern hemisphere it flows counter clockwise.) We will be spinning clockwise only the following chakras: Root chakra (1), Kundalini (2), Emotional Body (3), Heart chakra (4), Throat (5), Third eye (6) and Crown (7). Our research has shown that the auric field contains the complete spectrum of frequencies of light from red to blue violet to white. Each chakra can also exhibit the full spectrum although there is a tendency for a chakra to show a prevailing frequency band that is, have a particular color. The lower chakras are marked by colors lower in the light spectrum and therefore, lower frequencies. Higher frequencies and colors higher in the spectrum characterize the upper chakras.

## VORTEX SPINNING INFORMATION

Spinning chakra vortices clockwise is often as confusing as identifying which is your right or left side. Here are simple instructions.

❖ While lying on your back imagine that your chakras two through six are clocks with the face pointing toward the ceiling. Twelve o'clock is toward your head and six o'clock is toward your feet.

❖ When you spin your chakras clockwise, visualize starting at twelve o'clock while creating a circle to the left, then down, to the right and then up.

❖ If you have difficulty use your finger to circumscribe the circle above your body.

❖ Visualize your root chakra (1) facing toward your feet. Twelve o'clock is at your pubis and six o'clock is toward your tail bones.

❖ To spin your chakra clockwise visualize starting at twelve o'clock by creating a circle toward your left leg, down toward the floor, then upward toward the right leg and back to the pubis.

❖ Use your finger to circumscribe this circle which is projecting inward into your pelvis rather than downward to the surface you are lying on, as in the second through the sixth chakras.

❖ Visualize your crown chakra pointing away from your body. Twelve o'clock is the front of your head and six o'clock is at the back.

❖ To spin this chakra clockwise, visualize starting at twelve o'clock by creating a circle toward your right ear, down toward the back of your head and upward to your left ear and on to your forehead.

✤ Use your finger to circumscribe this circle which is projecting downward through the brain to the spinal cord.

✤ Imagine each chakra vortex like a funnel, large at the body surface and small as it approaches the spine.

✤ If the circle in any chakra is rough or irregular and the color is not clear continue the exercise longer.

✤ When there are major blocks, it may take several sessions to retrain a chakra to a circular vortex.

## SPINNING CHAKRAS

✤ Start by focusing on the root or the deep pelvic chakra, coloring it a rich red. If you don't see red, imagine a red apple, a red dress or a tie. See the energy spinning clockwise. Spin the chakra for at least ten complete revolutions. If it moves smoothly and easily in a complete circle a few repetitions will suffice. If it is stuck and resistant or moves in a lopsided circle, if it doesn't move or it goes counterclockwise and if the color fades, you need to spend more time and focus your awareness on this chakra, for there is a block in the vortex of the field.

✤ Next move to the lower abdomen, the kundalini. Color it orange and spin it clockwise ten circles, while you observe the spinning. In our culture this chakra is often weak with a poor flow.

✤ Now focus on the solar plexus, the emotional body; color it yellow like a lemon. Spin it clockwise ten times.

14

✤ Next be aware of the heart chakra; color it green --- a rich, vibrant green, like new growth in the Spring. Spin the chakra ten times clockwise.

✤ Now be aware of your throat; color it a rich yet light blue, like a clear sky. Spin it clockwise ten times. As you progress upward in the body, the colors become lighter and more vibrant, approaching the frequencies of white.

✤ Next focus on the third eye; see it as a light violet, orchid or lavender color. Spin it clockwise ten times. You will note as you move up the body the vortex becomes smaller and it spins faster.

✤ Finally pay attention to the crown chakra, visualizing it as a crystal clear white, like water or ice. Image spinning the chakra clockwise with the vortex going deep down into the body. Spin it ten times or until it spins freely.

✤ Because all momentum slows down over time, go back to each of the chakras in sequence, visualizing the corresponding color and spinning them several times. Start with the red root chakra, then on to the orange kundalini, the yellow emotional body, the green heart chakra, the blue throat chakra, the violet third eye and the white crown.

✤ Now lie there quietly and visualize energy flowing from your feet upward in each chakra toward the crown, where it flows up and out and spills down around your body in a white light.

# ❧⊘ Summary & Conclusions ⊘❧

With practice, breathing through the chakras and spinning them with color will become automatic and take less time. Now you can move on to other meditations. Those of you with major energy problems may continue these physical exercises as your primary or total meditation for some time.

These skills to activate chakras and the energy field flow are basic to Mind Mastery. Expanded consciousness encompasses a complete spectrum of vibrations from grounding in the lower frequencies (red - orange) combined with power in the middle frequencies (yellow - green) and great power in the higher frequencies (blue - white). Higher evolution requires a smooth flow through all chakras and areas of the body. Additionally as your field becomes more coherent you can expect a refined physiology that improves healing.

I encourage you not to make the mistake of shortening this training so you can rapidly move on to more exciting meditations. Each chapter provides skills that you need to master before moving on to the next set of meditations.

16

# Chapter 3
#  OPENING EMOTIONS

$W$e have demonstrated the direct relationship between emotion and the mind field's vibrational patterns. To heal and to evolve require that we be able to coherently organize our emotional energy and expand the mind field (see *Infinite Mind* - Chapter VIII). This chapter describes how to gain these skills.

You will learn to find the source of unsuccessful emotional patterns embedded in your memory from childhood and other lifehood experiences. The Mind Mastery Meditations will help you to gain a new appreciation of your emotional energy and a growing freedom to experience it - to better understand why your energy is misused and to eliminate blocks to emotional enjoyment and problem solving.

During expanded states of consciousness, emotions flow on a continuum from subconsciousness to everyday awareness to superconsciousness, each with a different connection to superconsciousness. Superconsciousness states have been viewed as altered states because we have believed that arbitrary breaks occur between consciousness levels. However, from a more enlightened wholistic perspective, "altered states" describe only a blockage in the consciousness continuum not an inevitable condition.

Most psychotherapeutic techniques deal with ordinary and subconscious levels of awareness. Transpersonal psychology now is concerned with ordinary to super-consciousness states. Such emphasis points out that the greater blocks lie in the transitions between ordinary and sub --- and superconsciousness. We have learned to separate these special awarenesses from everyday ones. Both ends of the consciousness continuum contain emotional energy. The subconscious level deals with material existence and drives. The superconsciousness state is concerned with spiritual life. We generally consider our destiny to be connected to material-physical happenings. However, the primary destiny which brings us back lifetime after lifetime is the spiritual destiny which is tied to higher states of consciousness and emotions.

Emotions and imagery are different in super --- and subconsciousness states depending on the condition of consciousness at the time. During ordinary reality emotion is powerful, materially oriented to self, body, possessions and the values we place on them. If emotion is either repressed or hyper-stimulated, physiological responses occur which over time can bring on psychosomatic repercussions. Basic emotions are organized to protect our perceptions of material reality. The imagery and daydream states of ordinary reality are of the real "now" world even if the material is symbolic. The colors visualized are dark or rich.

In contrast, the emotions of the superconscious state are love, ecstasy, and include divine experiences with God symbols, teachers and wise guides. There are air and water symbols, light in color and etheric in quality. The physiological systems are quiescent and operate in low normal ranges. If the state is prolonged or habitual the lack of physiological stimulus brings on deficiency diseases. The superconscious states are like daydreaming or fairy tales. In our culture these entertain us but are not easily believed or valued. Yet the experiences we remember most are peak experiences coming from superconscious states.

These extremes of consciousness seem distant from each other and linked only by ordinary reality. But like a circle made by two actions that each take the opposite direction, these states are strongly bonded together by emotions. On one end the function of emotions is to protect and save the body, and on the other end to protect and embellish the soul.

With such important goals we erect stubborn defenses against uncovering the deep sources of emotional disturbances. Without more sub --- and superconsciousness information we can only struggle to solve emotionally charged problems.

Emotion is aroused energy --- a human power source which is intrinsically neither bad nor good. Unpleasant problems highlight your cursory thoughts about emotions. You may experience confusion and frustration because you can't seem to get ahead or solve a problem. Generally the real problem is isolated by the closed emotions of ordinary reality. When considering ordinary behavior, things that happen to disturb you are more the result of your emotional dynamics than a direct response to anything happening in your external world.

But what is the general source? To experience the potential loss of your life or the destruction of your soul brings intense emotions that you are unable to understand, to dissipate or eliminate. Therefore, you literally "shut away" your memory of an actual event while you dissipate the emotional energy with physical hyperactivity, nervous tension or psychosomatic disturbances. These behaviors are predictable by the huge gaps that appear in the energy field frequencies and in the consciousness continuum.

Defenses are a part of all ordinary consciousness but they do not exist in higher states. The memory of the experience that caused the emotional turmoil is held in higher consciousness while the defenses are created in ordinary awareness to protect you from the strong emotions and frightening experiences. The memory of the original experience is protected by repressive blocks, which have now become disconnected residuals that get in the way of your evolution.

By focusing attention upon defenses psychotherapy literally nourishes them. The harder you consciously try to eliminate defenses the tougher they become. Defenses are best eliminated by literally side-stepping them. Acknowledge your defenses while you ask yourself if you are tired of this behavior, your blocks, and if you are ready to give them up. Answers to such questions actually weaken the boundaries of defenses. Remember you created these and only your resolute decision can eliminate them.

There is but one goal with Mind Mastery Meditations, to help solve the soul's unfinished business. You do this by developing power and security by knowing who and what you are on the soul level and by manifesting this greatness as a living human being. At the first level this constitutes expansion and integration of consciousness. The material problems of finances, social relations and ego strength are connected only as detours and troublesome sub-problems that will be solved by better everyday choices, whereas large problems relegated to the wisdom of higher consciousness will cause a major "phase shift" in your evolution.

The following Mind Mastery Meditations have been tested to fulfill the following objectives:

To give you skill in opening the mind-field.
To weaken defenses and to expand the consciousness on a continuum.
To give you comfort and command over free flowing emotions.
To recover authentic information from the source about your non-adaptive
    patterns (see Chapter IV).

Some meditative philosophies insist that you give up "self." I don't request that, for I wish you to become acquainted with higher, regular and lower levels of self. Consult yourselves to insure that no one in particular has absolute command over the others.

When you first embark on your path of self discovery reevaluate this common attitude, "I must hurry to get it over with." You will never complete your ultimate growth until you have embarked upon changing your relationship to the world by changing your relationship to yourself.

## EMOTIONS

Most people in our culture experience limited emotional resources. They are acquainted only with their own staid repertoire of emotions. Their only referent is how they handle their own emotional energies. Pure anger, love and fear are generally watered down, misplaced into generalized affect states of anxiety and sadness mixed with feelings of insecurity, unworthiness and distrust. Often the mind is unable to direct this energy because it doesn't understand why and from where it originated. With no clear course of action the mind frequently dampens this energy source.

The primary task then in the Mind Mastery of emotions is to allow yourself to experience from a higher source while being sufficiently grounded so as not to get lost in turmoil. In this expanded state you can acknowledge and recognize what it is that activated the emotions. You will realize that the actual stimulus is not the source situation --- it is a trigger. And you will understand that emotions don't occur independently. You established a pattern of what activates emotions and how you defuse or express these. It is nearly impossible to eliminate emotions intellectually. Curbing them is psychologically and medically unwise. Rampant emotional expression is socially unacceptable. However, it is imperative that you free the bound emotions so that you can learn to direct the energy toward the evolution of yourself and others.

19

The starting point is to consciously describe to yourself realistically the emotions which upset you and are unresolved as well as those which make you feel secure. Honestly survey your pattern of yourself. Acknowledge "this is how I am." What about it bothers you the most? Are you ready to give up this unsuccessful pattern while remembering that these are defenses which cover up pure and stronger emotions you haven't liked? Before you start the following emotional exercises, ask yourself if you are willing and able to recall some of the highly emotional episodes which you may have forgotten.

## ACCESSING THE MIND FIELD

*I*f you can see images spontaneously when you close your eyes and relax, move on. If you are not skilled in visual imagery continue with the following exercises. Remember that you are constantly imaging as you daydream or think. But you need to become more skilled in remembering these images. This is the most important initial tool in Mind Mastery. You must know what is going on in your mind to skillfully manage or change it. If you sidestep this skill, you will not remember your profound experiences when you return to ordinary states of consciousness. Mind Mastery also insures that your "will," personality and ego do not direct your meditations or your major decisions. Your guidance will come from a divine level.

✤ Ground yourself by breathing through your left foot, up and across your lower back and out your right foot to the ground.

✤ Briefly breathe through your chakras and spin them.

✤ Imagine that your own television set is turned on and you are watching your minds' passing stream of events. You may see the pictures projected out in front like a television set, or pictures behind your eyes.

✤ As you watch your pictures, if there is a story, an elaborate theme, or bits and pieces of a picture, monitor what is happening but don't get involved in the story line or spontaneous emotion. You are only seeking information.

✤ If the picture fades and a new one does not take its place, command the image to return but don't struggle to see it.

**20**

## IMAGERY EXERCISES

✤ Ground yourself by the tether line exercise.

✤ Increase the flow of energy by breathing through the chakras and raise the body's frequency level by spinning chakras.

✤ Close your eyes; turn on your personal television set to your minds' passing stream of events. Visualize yourself walking on a path or a road. If no path appears, see yourself walking until a road or ground appears under your feet.

✤ Observe what it is and where it is going. If you find yourself in the sky or flying, look down and follow a road somewhere.

✤ Casually look around and see the landscape, the plants, trees and any buildings or people who may appear. Take in the entire scene.

✤ Let your stream of consciousness unfold. Do not interpret, only observe and record in your mind-field memory.

✤ If you come to water, look in and see yourself or a picture. Water represents your mystical nature. Stay with the picture, letting it flow like the television images.

✤ Stop walking now, but with your eyes closed, recall what happened, as though you were telling someone. The skill of remembering requires placing imagery in the brain memory banks.

# SUGGESTIONS

✿ Do this exercise of imaging your mind's passing stream of events each day when you start your meditation session. This is a good consciousness warm-up exercise, where the soul level of self is close by.

✿ To vary your imagery start with guided imagery. Recall a beautiful scene you have encountered in the past. Ask to remember the colors, the odors, and the emotions. These sensations will become integrated into your imagery.

✿ The information or images may have no rhyme nor reason. At this stage, you are learning to pay attention to information from the mind. If you try hard to see the images or to make cognitive sense out of these images, they generally stop. The key words are allow and pay attention.

✿ If you get a black screen just stare at the screen and wait for your mind to warm up. Don't try to force pictures to happen. Color, lines, spots, swirls or geometric designs may occur first. Casually observe these until they grow into recognizable shapes.

✿ When you spread your focus over the entire screen you may see action at the edges of the screen but not in the middle. If you have not seen visual images easily before, these partial images are a prologue to future imagery. Color imagery indicates strong emotional energies.

✿ If you have thoughts during the imagery, be able to describe them, but be sure not to interpret them. Be non-judgmental and separate yourself from the content of the pictures until the pictures flow freely.

21

✿ If you try to decode "gem information" immediately you loose its deeper meaning. I encourage you to recall these gem experiences but to file them on the shelf for storage and eventual contemplation. The real meaning will come to you later in some quiet moment --- with a spontaneous "ah-ha."

#  INSTRUCTIONS

## ADDITIONAL IMAGERY EXERCISE

✤ There are many trips you can take to gain inner information and discover deeper meaning. Practical trips include walking up a long set of stairs to see who you meet at the top or accepting a gift and unwrapping it to discover a story.

✤ More mystical trips include climbing a hill and looking off into space. Walk on path to anywhere.

✤ Think of yourself as a glowing candle radiating light which draws all things to it. Observe yourself in this radiance.

## FIND A SMALL CHILD

✤ Start again on your path following the previous suggestions; you should have even richer imagery.

✤ Again check your relaxation. See if your field is out around your body. Notice the color of the field.

✤ Start walking again but with no particular destination. The path may be the same or a different one.

✤ This time you will find a small child. Note such things as what the child is wearing? What does the child look like and what is his approximate age? Take his or her hand and let the child lead you. The child has something to show you; you are the passive one. The child knows where to go; you will follow. You may inquire where the child is taking you but don't expect a specific answer. Let this go on for as long as the imagery progresses.

✤ Now spend a few moments to recall what you saw or heard with the child and your feelings. You may have more elaborate or additional imagery as you recall; let these images continue. Allow whatever happens to happen. Oftentimes sharing your imagery with friend is helpful. But do not analyze or explain your imagery.

22

# SUGGESTIONS

❀ Some people bring in beautiful pleasant pictures, others ugly, morose and scary ones. The mind-field contains both kinds. What came was evidence of some unfinished business. Don't focus the emotions on what you saw. At this stage you are not to judge, only to observe. Each imagery exploration will help you to uncover your unfinished emotional business.

❀ Note whether you saw colors and if these were light or dark. The light shade of higher spectrum colors represents the superconscious state and the deeper, richer colors the sub-conscious part.

❀ Many people see animals, a basic symbol of emotions. If the animals were ugly or unpleasant they represent the uncomfortable emotions of anger or fear. If soft, cuddly or happy animals, these represent the pleasant emotions. As children we project our feelings onto animals and pets and as adults these continue subconsciously. Note whether your animals were grounded, flying or swimming. This tells us something about your state of consciousness when you had those images and how you handle emotions.

❀ Some people find buildings or houses either open or locked. Try to enter to see what's inside. Peek in a window or walk around and find an open door. The house of course, represents you, your emotional house.

❀ Sometimes a barricade occurs on the path. Don't try to tear it down because another will appear to replace it. It indicates a resistance to knowing. Find a way around it or turn and go another way. Ask yourself if you are really ready to see what is on the other side. If you are, the barrier will dissolve.

23

❀ If you see a sign, read it. If you get a package, open it or ask what's in it. All of these are the mind's way of being cautious and only giving you a peak in here and there. Be patient. You are learning to know yourself.

❀ If you see a dramatic symbol ask for more information as to what this represents to you. Let the information stimulate more imagery.

❀ If your path splits, don't reason which is the better fork. Be intuitive; take the one you want or the first one that appears.

❀ Pay attention to any people who come into your imagery. Note what you feel about them. Make their acquaintance. Ask them what they want to tell you.

❀ During this exercise when ordinary consciousness expands into super or subconsciousness, we often forget the images. To establish a permanent memory in the brain you need to practice imagery recall.

# ❦INSTRUCTIONS❧

✤ Ground yourself and concentrate upon physical relaxation. Breathe through all your chakras from your feet through your head. Spin the upper seven chakras with color.

✤ Bring in your child or a guiding figure but remember that you are in charge and that they go along just for company or security.

✤ Allow yourself to spread out in all levels of consciousness.

## HAPPINESS

✤ Recall your happiest experience in this lifetime. Several may pop into mind. Intuitively accept one experience even if you don't remember it well.

✤ Allow yourself to be the person in that experience. How old were you? See the place where it occurred. What was the time and the year? Who was there with you?

✤ Allow all memories to flood your consciousness uncensored - feel the excitement. Continue with your imagery until the story has terminated or until the happiness changes to another emotion.

✤ Now ask the question: "Have I ever had a similar emotional experience earlier in this life or in another lifehood?"

✤ If new imagery and emotions appear, passively follow both. Don't become personally involved but do sense if it's the same pattern of handling emotions or a new one.

✤ If pleasant emotions change to uncomfortable ones, ask the question: "What happened to change my emotions? Do I have a pattern of anxiety when I experience unabridged happiness?"

✤ When you have finished every emotional episode, recall all the details and allow more information to come to you.

✤ If your experience was pleasant, you may recall the experience whenever you begin meditation. If it becomes too unpleasant, delay the imagery for a later time.

## PAIN OR FEAR

✤ Prepare your energy field for a meditation experience.

✤ Recall the most painful or frightening experience you have had in this or another lifehood. This imagery is often difficult to uncover because of the uncomfortable emotions which surface.

✤ If your memory is blank, ask if it occurred at birth, during a near drowning or suffocation, with anesthetic or injury or death at the hands of humans.

✤ In the beginning try to locate your awareness above the experience, as though you are seeing but not struggling with what happened.

✤ You will return to that experience many times until emotional freedom occurs and the information becomes more complete.

24

# SUGGESTIONS

✿ These emotional exercises are discussed early in the book because emotional freedom is so important for the remaining meditations. Repeating these emotional exercises will help clarify the changes that you need to make.

✿ Actually all other Mind Mastery skills are easier than straightening out old emotional patterns.

✿ If you discover that you condemn yourself for unacceptable emotional patterns know that these are defenses. Be honest --- this is how you are. You learned this pattern when it was the best adjustment you could make. Now it is no longer acceptable. Formerly you made a decision to change these habits. If the pattern keeps recurring become angry with the pattern, not at yourself.

✿ You may find that the rational level of your consciousness immediately excuses you by saying that so-and-so made me do it, or my culture encourages such behavior. Immediately drop these defenses; you cannot escape the problem by laying blame on something. You must change. Regardless of how the emotional patterns occurred, you are stuck with an unacceptable way of handling emotions.

✿ But do not repress anger because you were powerless to change a situation. For emotional growth we are not concerned with a realistic outcome. We are only concerned with understanding and changing repressed emotions.

✿ If in actuality you could not change a situation your body may have suffered greatly. But if you did not stand up for yourself and express your strong feelings, your soul suffered more. An unresolved soul tragedy is the deepest source of man's emotional restrictions.

✿ I have asked you to get in touch with your emotions of fear and pain but closely connected is the protective emotion of anger which many of us fear the most.

✿ Anger musters courage to take action to get out of the situation or to confront the situation that created the fear.

✿ You must recognize that by successful confrontation you grow in strength and security and the threat lessens.

✿ As you gain the ability to assert your value and your rights - what you will not tolerate, as well as the inexcusable mistakes of others that affected your life - you will take command of your emotions and your anger will dissipate naturally.

✿ Remember how we handle emotions and where we place them determines our behavior and the quality of our lives.

✿ Once you have started this process of experiencing emotions and asking for information, the process will become automatic in your daily life. When intense emotions occur, you will be able to clarify whether the current situation is exaggerated by old unresolved emotional patterns.

# LOVINGNESS

*T*he major emotional problems of our culture today are connected with love. We all know love based on the deep emotional experiences our love feelings bring us. Love problems start early in life, even in utero. A healthy, full term child born into a family who wants him, of a mother who has relished the opportunity of her pregnancy by fully participating in his growth and birth is programmed to love. Not everyone is so fortunate. But in addition, each child brings his soul's prior memories of love to start this life with either affection debits or credits. We carry love memories of this life in our brain and of other lifehoods in our field.

Quickly we learn to connect pleasant or unpleasant experiences with those humans who feed and care for us. They are the recipients of our emotions of love. Our love experiences now have a human object which gives us love or removes it. When we anchor our love with people, love can be bartered. We believe that we will be loved if we behave the way others want, and be unloved if we behave differently. Over time we associate love feelings with objects that comfort or make us secure --- our sex, race, ethnic group or nation, and with our valued possessions... our house, cars, children and animals. We withdraw love from those who differ.

As time passes love can become fully depersonalized, very encapsulated and encumbered when we believe that others have control over our love experiences. Ideally, to handle love problems we should be able to erase all negative connections. Some meditation systems claim to do this. I doubt it. For those who claim to have removed love barriers without personally changing I find their expression of love to be insipid and ungrounded with bland, uninspired emotions. These Mind Mastery Meditations point to love as a pleasant, exciting experience in the mind-field with coherent, smooth flowing energy. There is no material recipient; it is a God given feeling state which is truly unconditional. In Mind Mastery Meditations we can learn to reclaim our love emotions as our own, not others. Here we do not primarily love objects or people; we have a profound emotional experience of lovingness. Here emotion is clear and pure without the baggage and blocks that have previously encumbered our emotions.

Lovingness as a feeling is very personal; as an object it is highly impersonal in that you don't receive love, you just manifest lovingness. It is a field phenomena which does not belong to a chakra or to the heart. A loving field permeates all bodily cells; it radiates outward in the aura to contact other fields. It expands and becomes billowy with the divine high frequencies of white combined with low, life-giving frequencies of red; the color is a glowing pink. All happy babies and adults show pink auras when they experience lovingness.

26

27

# SUGGESTIONS
## LOVINGNESS MEDITATION

❖ Relax your body and physically manipulate your chakras.

❖ Sit with your eyes closed. Image the pure form of lovingness, pink in color, deep within your tissue and radiating outward. You may easily recall the time you sensed your greatest lovingness. Let lovingness overshadow any prior frustration with love feelings; now there is no recipient and there are no consequences. The warm delight of lovingness is yours to experience and enjoy. Take your time.

❖ You will feel your vibrations increasing smoothly or with sudden jump-ups, as you encounter a "phase shift." Your aura will grow like an inflating balloon until it spills over and fills your meditation place.

❖ When your field gets too big for the room and building let it expand through walls, windows, doors and roof. This subtle energy has no barriers. See your field hovering like a pink cloud over your building.

❖ Stop the lovingness expansion now and experience your gigantic, marvelous lovingness energy manifest. It should feel better than good; it is delicious.

❖ When you are ready, return your consciousness to your meditation location but do not bring back your loving energies - let them hover in space. Note that your field is now identical to your expanded lovingness but is only smaller in size. Focus on this for a few minutes.

28 ❖ Now return your awareness to the room where your imagery started and eventually to your physical body. The energy remains where you projected it; only your awareness is now more local. Recognize your warm glow. Now go about your day with a divine lovingness "hang over".

# ❀❀ SUGGESTIONS ❀❀

✿ Lovingness is not limited to a specific time and space; it can only be expanded and retracted. Don't be concerned about where this energy comes from or if it will run out. The energy is inexhaustible, reprogrammed from the fields of others and the universe.

✿ Be aware that although you don't pinpoint this energy it is available as a field to all humans and animals in despair or in need of lovingness. Be cognizant that it radiates both outward from and inward toward your tissues and self. Enjoy it and let it set you free.

✿ Remember that as you gain skill to experiencing lovingness you will realize that this energy and these feelings are available to you at all times, for fun and for changing unpleasant emotions to glorious ones.

# Summary & Conclusions

All information about past experiences and habitual patterns from any lifetime are available to you at any time if you become skilled at opening and monitoring the stream of events in the mind-field. Opening the mind-field is the first giant step in Mind Mastery, the soul's unavoidable journey. With skill, you can on command, access the mind-field information by asking a question and awaiting the answer. You will get answers, whether you like them or not. You will gain comfort and command over your free flowing emotions and you will have the opportunity to change old outmoded emotional patterns. Remember that the primary blocks in your evolutionary process are emotional and hidden. This series of sequential meditation techniques can open the mind-field and let your everyday consciousness look in and become enlightened.

32

# Chapter 4
##  UCOVERING LIFEHOODS

Current literature on reincarnation is repete with outmolded concepts about karma that were formulated in ancient cultures. At that time ways of thinking about the nature of the human in his universe were limited. There are many who have accepted reincarnation and karma blindly; others often reject the whole concept because it is surrounded by irrational, unintelligent justifications and beliefs. At one time these karmic beliefs served to explain on a simplistic level what man observed and experienced about previous lifehoods. Yet now with our greater understanding of human behavior and emotions these beliefs based upon predestination are limiting to our concepts of self-determined evolution. Karma based upon so called "natural laws" of the universe are like the older "universal laws" from physics. When reexamined through particle physics and energy field concepts these "universal laws" are not unalterable truths. At best both are relative to limited material situations.

Just as it took thousands of years to change the idea that the earth was flat we can expect that old beliefs about karma will also linger. However, let's not throw out the divine concepts of reincarnation with the outmoded concepts of karma. Reincarnation is a fact and it is divine. Karma and the old explanations of it are not. There are skilled psychics who claim to channel past lives. In tracing certain personality characteristics or current problems, some psychics seem to be able to read answers from the fields of others and to eliminate some stresses. As a short term goal this is extremely helpful. It may be effective for people who wish to work on an isolated problem, yet these readings are often incorrect and of little significance except as interesting stories that are difficult to integrate into one's life. Someone else cannot do it for us. If you want the greatest growth and evolution from lifehood information you must discover and relive your own lifehoods. Furthermore, the greatest good comes from the changes you make not from the information you receive.

When you discover lifehood information you will see some similarities with your present life because it is the same soul. But it is inaccurate to think that your past lives will provide answers to your current problems. There is never a cause and effect correlation between past lives and current problems. Generally the cause of the problem lies elsewhere. Psychoanalytic procedures reveal that there are five or six levels of partial answers, each giving some symptomatic relief. But when you no longer need to intellectually understand or explain the problem, it is gone. If you believe you no longer have a problem because you intellectually understand, for example, why your parents behaved as they did and you forgive them, you don't understand the problem. Only when you have seen your role in your unfinished business of this and past lives, and have changed, will the problem dissolve, rather than being superficially solved.

Some people say that they don't want to delve into past lives to learn painful things. They would rather live in the present and the future. What they fail to recognize is that past experiences are still with the soul which is now in a new physical body. Awareness does not change the facts but it does give us skills to connect all levels of consciousness by opening the blocks in the mind-field.

Why can't people remember lifehoods if they actually lived them? Children easily remember then but adults have built up emotional barriers to knowing. Let me summarize my beliefs with the following prose:

### LIFE OF LIVES

The strongest human beliefs arise from the profound invisible reality of God. No man can become self-realized without belief in his immortal soul.

The fulfilling of human destiny depends upon what we have become aware of and what our soul has done with it.

And yet, forgetfulness dims our early remembrances of this life and a body veil of secrecy seems to hide other life experiences as if to insure that this life remains the soul's primary concern.

The truism, to know thyself will set you free, is unattainable until awareness of the unfinished business of childhood expands to include the incomplete work of lifehoods.

Then, as man's level of awareness, his consciousness, is fed by this inner knowing, he can command the full spectrum of his existence. Only then can he realize truth, and his soul be freed to exercise his will as the divine will of God.

As Leo Tolstoy wrote "A life is but one of the dreams of the more real life and so it is endless until the last one, the very real life, the life of God."

34

We have established that the mind is not in the brain or nerves --- it is a field. And if the past influences one's present life, it must be by way of the mind-field. The mind which experiences is different from the brain which records. To be in touch with repressed experiences of this and past lives we must literally move our awareness out of our heads and into the mind-field which originally recorded the experience. Opening the mind-field to recover past life, earlier life and what is going on now is a skill which can be learned. Early in this life we closed the doors of the mind field to protect us from remembering difficult experiences, or our destiny which fostered our reincarnation.

Follows are some powerful experiences to help you extend your stream of consciousness into all important lives that you have lived toward ultimately learning your paramount lessons. These experiences help you to gain skill in opening your mind-field at will and recovering past experiences by yourself. But before progressing to lifehoods you need to gain skill in imaging your current life both by free and structured imagery.

# INSTRUCTIONS

## THIS LIFE - AGE REMEMBERING IMAGERY

❖ First ground yourself using one of the techniques in chapter two. Then relax your body and activate your field by breathing.

❖ Next, see yourself on a high mesa overlooking a grand and beautiful valley below. This entire valley is all yours; you're going down to claim it. There is a safe path with gradual inclines and steps with firm hand rails. Start your trip down toward your valley. Take your time and notice the imagery that appears. Pay attention to what you see as you walk without understanding what the pictures mean.

❖ When you reach the bottom, sit quietly and absorb the valley essences. When you're ready, create your house within the valley. Take your time. Pay attention to what you envision as your place. When it is completed go within to be with your deepest self --- to commune with your soul. Stay as long as you wish. When you return to ordinary consciousness, recall the experience as though you were telling it to a friend.

❖ As you quietly relax in your peaceful valley reminisce about your current life. Ask to see an image of yourself from between ages 12 and 15. When the picture comes pay attention to what you are wearing, where you are, who is with you, the time of year and what you are doing. Let the image progress to a party, school or a social setting. Follow the image until the program stops or you tire of the image. Stop imaging and recall what happened and your feeling state at this time. By remembering you are placing the imagery in your brain and dissolving any schisms between levels of your consciousness.

❖ Allow that picture to fade. Now you will see an image of yourself between the ages of 8 and 11. What's on your mind? What are you doing? What are you wearing? If your imagery brings up experiences that you remember, follow these. If you recall any specific incident that happened at that time, remember it. Don't hurry to get to the next meditation. This one may take your entire meditation time.

❖ Erase the last picture and see yourself as you were sometime between the ages of 4 and 7. You are the same person just younger. How old are you? What are you doing? What are your thoughts? If you have difficulty seeing any particular age group, ask again to see yourself as that age and be patient.

❖ Now, wipe your mental screen clean and bring in a new image of yourself as a very little one between ages 1 and 3. Are you happy? Do you like this age? Do You have specific memories? Stay with these images as long as you wish.

❖ Next see yourself as a new born baby. Are you happy or sad? Ask why and await the answer. If you chose to be born now, why is this a special time for you? What is your destiny? When finished recall your imagery.

❖ Stop imaging and open your eyes slowly. Imagine that you are telling an interested friend about your imagery and what happened. Don't try to interpret the images. This is an exercise in recording these experiences from the higher mind to the brain so that on command you can recall them.

36

# SUGGESTIONS

✿ If pictures are slow to appear there are probably emotional experiences which temporarily block your imagery. Again, when your imagery comes follow it. If emotion comes ask to see what happened to cause your feelings.

✿ It is acceptable to visualize a photo of yourself at various ages. Photographic imagery is a little more hidden --- it protects you from re-experiencing that time in your life, but it does bring information from the same source.

✿ Sometimes these exercises are called regression techniques. I call them remembering because you are experiencing a memory of those events in the present. You are not an infant or an 8 to 10 year old. You are your present age recalling stored information.

✿ You will be amazed that your linear brain will find it so easy to remember what you thought you had forgotten. Don't forget that all experiences are first recorded in the mind and are therefore always available to you.

✿ Recall which age was the most difficult to image. Spend more time later with that age which is blocked by emotional secrets. The exercises which I have given you were to open the mind-field memories of this life but if from the questions you go deeper, you will recall lifehoods as real as when they were lived. Like any physical, emotional or intellectual skill, you must practice to tune your capacity.

✿ If any one of these exercises has taken you on an extended experience, go back and repeat it in days to come. You may start with any interesting experience which is likewise unfinished but it is the bright, emotional ones that are the most important. The repetition of imagery also enhances your skill in contacting all mind-field information. You do not need to complete all the age groups at one time. If the imagery becomes real, stay with it and move to the next age group another time. Again, these are techniques that use this life's experiences to find the emotional blocks that were brought from other lifehoods.

37

✿ In summary the technique is simply to watch imagery and ask questions to allow the imagery to progress. When spontaneous emotion occurs, ask if it has occurred earlier in this life. If it has, ask to return to the earlier event to see it. Allow your imagery to continue in this new direction.

# INSTRUCTIONS

## THIS LIFE - PAIN, SURGERY, ILLNESS AND DISASTER

❖ As a small child did you ever have surgery which used inhalation anesthetic such as ether or gas?  If you have, hold that in your memory.  Were you ever hurt very much or very afraid?  Have you been seriously ill or nearly drowned?  Did you ever experience a disaster when you thought you would not live?

❖ Pick the experience that immediately stands out in your mind and allow yourself to drift back in real life to recall that experience.  You will be there consciously; it will all come back to you in the present time: the details of where you are, the people, the sounds and the odors.  This may be emotionally painful but you need to recover what happened.

❖ Allow the story to unfold while you are in touch with the accompanying emotion.

*38*

# SUGGESTIONS

✿ This meditation helps you to contact frightening and painful experiences through imagery. Know that your previous experience is now a memory that still influences your life.

✿ Recall all physical sensations and the nature of your emotions. Allow these to flow if you can. Be particularly aware of anger if the dangerous situation was created by another person.

✿ If you are very frightened don't push to disclose the entire experience. Remember that fear is protective and you may not be ready for the experience without someone to support you. Individuals differ considerably on this exercise.

✿ Recall that this is a meditation to help you gain skill. You are not required to solve any condition or problem. Later you will learn to release the charges on these experiences when you find out what has fueled these from other lifehoods.

# INSTRUCTIONS

## LIFEHOODS - AGE IMAGERY

*T*hese following exercises will help you extend your stream of consciousness into important lives you have lived.

✤ Remember the exercise during which you imaged various age groups. Recall the time of the greatest feeling and allow yourself to return to that experience. Don't try to get details again; you want to recover the feeling state.

✤ Ask yourself if you have ever had that same emotion at an earlier time in this life. If your answer is yes, ask to return to that time and experience the episode again. Continue imagining that series until the images repeat themselves.

✤ Next ask if this was the first time your soul ever experienced this feeling or a similar situation. If your answer is no ask to return to the memory and imagery which is connected. If this happens you have tapped into a lifehood that may be more emotional than this life's experiences. If this is your first lifehood, you may be hesitant. Don't consciously struggle to bring in the information. Try another day.

✤ If the story unfolds with information in imagery, words, thoughts and emotions stay with it as long as you wish. Remember to find out your sex, age, the country, and the approximate time in history.

✤ When that first lifehood has wained out ask that you spontaneously recall additional events in that life. See yourself as a child after that episode. Generally the first lifehood memory is emotional and dramatic, but the actual episode does not give you enough information to know how or why certain events occurred in that lifetime.

40

✤ Now ask that you return to a memory as a young boy or girl (whichever your sex in that lifetime). Ask to see your family, parents and siblings and the state of affairs in your family, ethnic group and the geographical location where you lived.

✤ Later follow the life to its termination. Can you categorize it as a passive or active life? Did you want to die to remove yourself from impossible situations or did you fight to the end? What were your emotional patterns?

✤ Slowly return to regular consciousness; spend some time remembering and writing down your experience. If you believe there is more to this story, you know the way and you can go there during another meditation time.

✤ During some later meditation when you believe you have reexperienced this lifehood ask if you have ever lived another lifehood with similar situations. You may find that you were of the other sex, at a different time in history and area of the world. If the experience is similar allow the information and imagery to open up to you. Each time you recall a new lifehood with similar characteristics you will find the pattern more deeply rooted in your present life.

✤ Find yourself moving back and forth between the present and the other lifehoods. Be aware that you are progressing in *Mind Mastery.*

❀ The reason you ask yourself questions is to bypass the brain's rational answers to seek instead answers from the mind. To ask the question or give the command means that the intent is focused and the energy of the "will" is elicited. This gives you higher answers and opens closed areas of the mind.

❀ While working at this depth, the images may be fuzzy at first. Don't struggle to clear them up. Be patient; they will improve. Remember if an episode starts, keep your critical analytic thoughts out of the imagery.

❀ If nothing much happens generally there are emotional blocks to protect you from reexperiencing the event. Often there is ambivalence. One part of your consciousness is eager to know. Another part doesn't want to. By your questions you planted a seed that frequently bursts forth in answers during daydreaming or during repetitive work when your defenses are down.

❀ Remember that the information you gain from lifehoods and the patterns of behavior you observe are not automatically eliminated simply because you remember them. They will change only when you become so tired of your defenses that you really want them gone. Then and only then will you stop encouraging and feeding these defenses. While you can't change what happened to you in another lifehood, you can change the effects upon you now. To do this you must rewrite the scenario more satisfactorily. This means that you see yourself asserting and changing behaviors at those times when you made judgmental errors or you behaved weakly. Confronting your behavioral patterns will occur as you begin to rewrite a new scenario of who you are.

*41*

❀ You may become fearful even contemplating change so that you want to leave lifehoods alone and slumbering. If you don't wish to pursue farther at this time, please don't. When and if your soul seems stronger and you return to those memories, you are probably ready to reexperience them with greater insight and begin to change.

❀ As you continue with this work, you are beginning to peel the memory onion. Don't become lost in the glamour of who you were. Also don't reject the drama because that creates the emotional charges. The more spectacular these experiences the more impact they had upon your soul. But the actuality of who you were is less important than what you did or did not do. These are the residuals --- the patterns that must be integrated and/or changed.

❀ You have embarked upon the journey of self-discovery through Mind Mastery Meditations. Uncovering lifehoods is the most direct route. Your memory of one lifehood may be short. Others may last for many months, as long as new information and insights are appearing. Often times you will return to a previously remembered short lifetime to gain in-depth information. The first time around you may have been less ready for profound insights. Don't be in a rush to complete a lifehood and leave the gems undiscovered.

❀ With successful recovery of initial lifehoods you are better equipped to understand the effects of family and culture upon your current beliefs. And you are more equipped to evaluate the cultural beliefs which caused you to adjust poorly to the circumstances.

## LIFEHOODS - IMAGERY FROM PAIN, TRAUMA, SURGERY AND ILLNESS

✤ Recall the imagery of your initial experience with intense pain, surgery or illness. Again remember the emotional experience only. It should be easier this time.

✤ Ask if you ever had another similar emotional experience earlier in this life. Await the imagery to gain more emotion. If this occurs it will add new information to the experience you first recovered. Now ask if a similar emotional situation ever occurred in another lifehood.

✤ Follow the procedures you used to stimulate other lifehoods. See what sex you are; what you are wearing; image the area of the world, the time in history and what was occurring. Bring in the people who were with you, even those who created the pain and the situation where the trauma occurred. Were you saved? Did you recover or did you die?

✤ Follow by imaging your life after that episode all the way to your death in that life. What were your thoughts about that life? Was there any insight that came with death?

✤ Return to present time and recall your imagery and experience. Again note the patterns of your emotions and behavior. Are these similar in this lifetime? Are you beginning to see the sources of your behavior, the unfinished business that this soul brought from many lifetimes which is manifest again now?

42

# SUGGESTIONS

✿ Lifehood recall takes place in the present. Regression techniques should not be applied to lifehoods where the information is metaphysically held in the mind-field. As such it is out of time and so is not available to regression. Regression can only open the neural memory of this life.

✿ Each time that you return from your imagery to ordinary consciousness recall the story. You may write or record your recall verbally to help you remember more details. Also additional details will come to you when you return to the same lifehood on another day. If your name in that life comes to you it personalizes your experience.

✿ Never judge recovered information until numerous lifehood recalls show recurring patterns. These patterns disclose the emotional blocks that you act out.

✿ The information that is so clear in higher states of consciousness you may doubt when you return to ordinary consciousness. Only when consciousness flows evenly along a continuum do these realities blend into one coherent sense of knowing.

✿ Along this line, how can you tell if the imagery and information is of a real lifehood or a symbolic one which your mind has created to give you bits of information but not too much? Your linear brain will argue that your images come from a book you have read or a television program you saw or a fable or myth you remembered.

✿ This is how you can differentiate the real from the symbolic. With real lifehoods there is hesitation in the imagery and memory; emotions may come so spontaneously that these block the image. There will be physical symptoms and intense and sudden mood changes. You may see animals. Memory is often stumbling and speech monotone. Insights are alarming --- you have ah-ha's and deja vu experiences.

43

✿ With fantasy imagery your narration is smooth and elaborate like reading a story that is removed from yourself. Frequently you greatly enjoy and get emotionally carried along by the story. You know you are creatively imagining. It is fun.

✿ Actually, these fantasies have some value. Your mind creates the imagery --- not someone elses. You have chosen to create a story that contains some truth but you distort it sufficiently to keep your feelings from thoroughly manifesting. This is protective but as long as you know it you are in fact touching the essence of a real lifehood.

# ❦⊚INSTRUCTIONS ⊙❧

## LIFEHOODS - IMAGERY FOR TRAVELING INWARD (1)

𝒫eople differ in which techniques open the mind-field to memories of lifehoods. Here are two other methods that may work if the first two suggestions did not or if you did not find emotional states in this life to trip off lifehoods. Your defenses to lifehoods may be extremely high or you may have accepted belief systems that mitigate the first two. These are two quite non-threatening techniques that may take you equally as far.

✢ Ground yourself and relax any physical tensions.

✢ Is there an area of the world that intrigues you where you have never lived in this lifetime? You now have an opportunity to go there. Or you may choose not to go to a specific area but rather to explore.

✢ A huge balloon is waiting to take you on a journey of discovery. Get aboard, excited about your new adventure. Slowly see yourself drifting upward, forward and off into the distance toward your destination. Don't be in a hurry; have a nice trip as you observe all around you and the earth below. Take as much time as you wish.

✢ When you are ready your ship will land slowly and you will find yourself in a new land. Ask if this is your destination or just a rest or fuel stop.

✢ Let the story unfold. Observe the terrain, the buildings, the people, their clothes and behavior; about what year it is and in what country or area has your ship come to rest. If there are people greet them and tell them you are on a quest of self discovery. Now see yourself no longer a tourist of this place but a resident.

*44*

✢ Let the story continue until it comes to an end or you become disinterested. You may wish to return at another time because you sense that you had actually lived there.

✢ Return to ordinary consciousness and recall your experience. It is not important whether what you experienced was true. Here you are gaining skill. Important, authentic information will stick and the incorrect or unimportant will drop from your memory.

## LIFEHOODS - IMAGERY FOR TRAVELING INWARD (2)

✢ Imagine building a bridge across a chasm or a canyon. When it is built walk across it into a new land. Again follow the imagery wherever it takes you. Ask the questions you have learned to ask in all lifehood imagery exercises. Observe and recall.

### OR

✢ Imagine going into a cave with a bright light. Observe the inside for animal or human signs --- note the shape and structure of all the sides that you can see. Some may be pleasant, others not. Follow until you find an exit. A person will be waiting to take you to a lifehood with information and unfinished business. Ask for the name of this person or guide and have a dialogue with him or her.

✢ Now spend a few moments to recall the images of where you have been during your trip. It is important that you recall, as well as simply experiencing the images. Oftentimes in recall the experience becomes more elaborate.

# SUGGESTIONS

✿ Because these imaginary places were consciously created they may lack the emotion and be less complete that those coming more spontaneously. However, if you ask the questions and follow some suggestions you can gain in skill and your mind-field may release profound information from your higher consciousness.

✿ If your imagery had details, emotions, feelings and a sense of reality, it was undoubtedly a lifehood recall. It is not important that you decide if everything you saw was true. One always doubts when one starts recovering lifehoods. It is a good sign. But as you continue moving into these consciousness states and recover information, you will know and all unimportant or incorrect information will drop out. If you are not really sure about this lifehood ask the quick question. Is it a real life? Remember if the answer is no, that does not mitigate the general information. It is your imagery --- real or imagined --- and you have created your imagery from your experiences.

45

# ❦ SUMMARY & CONCLUSIONS ❧

*T*hese were my goals for you as I led you through uncovering lifehoods. Explore these to evaluate your growth:

To obtain skill in moving back and forth through the continuum of consciousness so that you can choose and command your reality constantly.

To become comfortable and free in experiencing emotional energies and to use these successfully in your life and evolution.

To disclose your most dominant protective defense patterns so that they become weaker as you grow in strength.

To put you in touch with the unfinished business of lifehoods, understanding your realized strengths, uncovering the latent ones and redefining your choices.

To give you opportunities to change your relationship to the world thus redirecting your behavior and attitudes toward your full and complete evolution.

Experiences from these meditations should have shown you what you have been and the residuals which define what you are today. These experiences let you know where you have made tremendous changes and where you play the same old wornout tape. You must realize that you are more than any of your lifehoods. You are all of your lives highlighted by the emotional importance which you have assigned to each of them. You are what you have done with your capabilities and your self-imposed restrictions.

46      You may have been overwhelmingly surprised to learn that you are not simply an ordinary person of your current sex, age and experience. By bringing in your complex memory of other lifehoods you glimpse a destiny and a motivation far beyond the personality of the human being you define as yourself today.

The skills you have gained from *Mind Mastery Meditations* will not automatically remove your soul's painful experience and unsuccessful blunders (the best you could arrive at the time) but they do point out a way. You can rationally decide that you are no longer happy with old behavioral patterns which you replay unconsciously. You can alter your long standing scenario. With "will" you let these old patterns drop. Even such determination does not change you immediately. But each time you bring such behaviors to conscious awareness you can weaken their bonds. In due time these defenses are gone.

The Mind Mastery techniques I have presented are not designed to solve isolated problems but as you change, ordinary problems are more easily solved. I am more concerned with developing your capacity to move back and forth, at will, with information from present and past lifehoods. In this process you tap into that part of the soul that some still call the oversoul. Here as your true destiny is revealed, one you may have never contemplated, your life will take on meaning and excitement. And the disparate aspects of your soul can be integrated more smoothly into your current personality. I want you to be able to take hold of your own power and to know that you have the skill and divine guidance to evolve more rapidly without outside help.

If you have progressed toward these goals, gaining skill in Mind Mastery and becoming more evolved, we come to the final problem. In my work with many individuals of all faiths, both sexes and in a wide age range of different races and ethnic groups, some young souls and some old ones, I find a common problem when we uncover the deepest and the highest level. The problem is not a subconscious one, but a super-conscious one. Each person has had difficulty with God. In times of great stress and insurmountable problems, all people turn to God. If their questions are not answered, if God does not save them from their impossible situation, then doubt, anger and frustration occur. It is easier to be angry with ourselves which we perceive unworthy than to be angry with God for not loving us enough to save us. Because we formulate our self worth in a family context we frequently believe our negative self-worth was created by our parents. Our cultural milieu has also helped to formulate our self-worth but we have accepted the image as ours. Actually the deep problem is in our relationship with God. I believe that unless this problem is eliminated, no soul can reach its true destiny, to become one with God, or to become God manifest. I believe this is the ultimate problem of evolution that cannot be sublimated or circumvented. It can only be eliminated by recovering the first and subsequent experiences during which problems with God occurred. Finally, when errors in our judgment are understood, we have the opportunity to change, often beyond recognition, as the burden is lifted. Enhanced wisdom, creativity, higher consciousness and enlightenment are the end results.

47

48

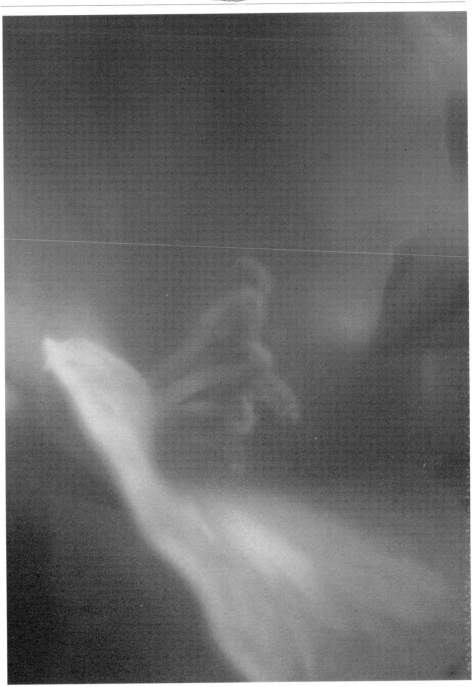

# Chapter 5
#  *HASTENING HEALING*

*T*his chapter presents information about the physical skill of self-healing. The physiology of healing is covered in my book ***Infinite Mind:*** *The Science of Human Vibrations.* Self-healing carries a two fold responsibility: (1) To remove all conditions known to lower our human resistances, including our lifestyle choices, and (2) to assume primarily responsibility for our health through our attitudes, practices and meditative skills. As we carry out these responsibilities we will hasten the body's healing response. Mind Mastery Meditations are geared to improving the fundamental unity of the body that heals and regenerates tissues in conformance with the body's intrinsic order.

Today allopathic medicine has no valid measure of health. Rather, health is an assumed ideal condition present in the absence of disease or known pathology. I describe health as a critically self-organizing biofield which allows for successful evolutionary adaptation in which the mark of health is a constantly self-healing organism. In other words, a healthy organism exhibits a flexible mind and accompanying plastic tissue systems. The general conditions of health show a coherent flexible relationship with self and the world. During disease and aging this resiliency is lost. It follows that piecemeal treatment of parts or tissues without considering overall health is doomed to have limited effects upon symptoms and no effect upon the total health. Health is also beyond any single state of consciousness; it is tied to the full continuum of consciousness, the realities of the mystical higher states, the everyday rational problem solving state and the reflex behavior of material tissue.

Medicine and the healing arts began together with the same personnel and philosophy. But in the 19th century medicine branched off from so-called art and took the path of biochemistry to discover life and define health. Despite major changes in physics which led away from the mechanical toward a more organismic view of life, medicine has not revised its direction. Biology and physiology also followed the reductionistic approaches. Throughout much of the 20th century medicine has been spectacularly successful with the use of the penicillin and sulfa drugs and their derivatives to handle infectious diseases. But the degenerative health problems, heart attacks, arterioscleroses, cancer, stroke, arthritis, ulcers and hypertension were less amenable to chemical treatment. This is when the ancient healing techniques from India, the Orient and the Native American Indians were introduced into Western treatment as viable and successful healing techniques. Shamanistic healing rituals became popular during the last part of this century.

At the same time some professionally trained physicians and scientists who recognized their mystical and visionary tendencies began to investigate the course of illness by studying energy rather than chemical treatments. They discovered that blood chemistry, believed to be the metronome of disease, failed to predict the course of disease. Physicians found that some persons with serious diseases who displayed creative receptivity to new ideas, flexibility and augmentation with strong egos, who expressed personal feelings of adequacy and vitality, lived longer than those passive people with an inactive immune system and uninvolved attitudes. Those with inner strength who knew how to fight apparently activated the life urge, hastening the body's healing response to recovery. These findings are tremendous testimonies of the importance of personal and emotional commitments for the healing of serious diseases. In a lesser degree these personal characteristics are requisite to all rapid recovery.

In my laboratory we discovered dimensions of the human energy field during illness and healing. We found that cancer patients who had no red color vibrations or the lower electromagnetic spectrum more often succumbed. Those with these lower field vibrations had good prognosis, remission or cure. If people could see red in their field or experience it in their bodies their healing capacity was accelerated. We learned that when human body frequencies become complex, coherent and flowing the body's physiology operates at maximum efficiency. Health is insured. But if the peak of complexity was exceeded the energy flow slipped toward chaos into anticoherency thus affecting the entire bodily chemistry. At these times the congenitally weaker systems failed. Chronic disease or dysfunction occurred. Such phenomena lead us to believe that the real source of chronic pain and illness, except traumatic injury, occurs first from energy field disorganization and only secondarily from some local tissue disturbance. There is a growing awareness that dynamic field interaction is the frontier view of health. Yet even with mounting evidence the old reductionist model appears again and again from researchers who state that each disease has its own energy field which must be reversed before healing can occur.

50   I would remind you that although some aspects of the field may be more disturbed than others, the problem of disease is a breakdown in the defenses of the body which is not localized to one part of the energy field. Specific disease treatment by either complementary field procedures or allopathic chemical ones can remove symptoms but will not provide health until health is restored to the entire field.

## ANCIENT HEALING TECHNIQUES

Let us survey some of the beliefs of the ancient priests and shaman chiefs who were assigned the role of healers of the tribe. Because of their close relationship to their people and their long observation and intimate sense of disease they have passed down much wisdom to the healers of today, particularly we who choose to be self-healers. What were their wisdoms? They always treated the whole body, including the highest level, the spirit. They saw disease as an imbalance where the power of the disease had temporarily overcome the power of the person. They learned that bacteria and disease became threatening where the body's protective field developed flaws. Their purpose was not to avoid death but to protect the soul and keep it intact while the weaknesses of the mind were aired and changed.

The great personal capacity of the shaman to move through all states of consciousness helped the healee and the tribe to loosen their bonds with perceived reality and flow with the body's intrinsic order. Information from the shaman to the ill person took place on a subconscious level. Shaman healers developed rituals to further insure that all levels of consciousness were available to the group to provide a profound energy source for empowering the ill one. Vivid imagination occurred in such group vibrations which assisted the healer in discovering the appropriate healing techniques for each person with each disease. The shaman's rapid and lucid shifting of reality encouraged the healer's field to become flexible and receptive to the field of treatments. Techniques from ancient healing arts all used higher states of consciousness to stimulate elaborate ecstatic imagination which produced vivid imagery.

Specific disease imagery was encouraged to combat troublesome symptoms but was always accompanied by field healing. Shamans frequently used physical and sensory deprivation such as sleeplessness, electrolyte imbalance, sexual abstinence, darkness, sacred hallucinogenic herbs and sound to encourage mystical states that faded the material body image.

## ENLIGHTENED HEALING BELIEFS

A new perspective has now emerged to assist us in designing appropriate self-help procedures. Health and disease are related not only to the chemical conditions of the cells and the atomic action of molecules upward but are controlled from above downward from the mental and emotional properties of the mind-field. Remember that the mind as a field is the first and primary contact of the bio-organism with the environmental fields. Both shamans and current researchers have hypothesized that all breaks in the body's integrity lie in problems of the person's relationship to himself and to the demands of the world as he sees them.

Current medical practitioners give the mind and emotions less recognition than do the spiritual and psychic healers who place primary emphasis upon healing the soul when it gets off track. These healers believe that forgetting who we are is the source of illness. Whereas outer healing of the body can temporarily save biological life only the inner healing of the belief systems and life choices can remove the contaminating source.

All self-healing procedures must take into account the person's emotional beliefs which inhibit or facilitate a positive attitude toward cure. Most important of these beliefs is the person's own "will" to recover. The positive and negative values that one has associated with illness or disease do affect recovery. Body drawing techniques can rapidly disclose these in detail. When disease is envisioned as a black demon-like entity that must be blasted, physically attacked or "dug out" the emotional energy is full of hate and distaste and does not encourage the healing response. Meditation teachers and healers often fall into the same trap by giving meditative images as though the disease can be eradicated only by poisoning, cutting or violent physically destructive acts. I believe this is entirely misguided. If the problem and its solution lie within the mind-field the energy should be used to engender powerful images of the strength of the self and soul and the "will" to stimulate the body's natural healing response to overcome the imbalance.

## CHECK YOUR HEALING BELIEFS

Before you begin to create helpful images for your self-healing, move into higher consciousness and ask yourself the following question: Am I totally ready to give up all needs for the disease? To be valid the answer must come from the higher state not from the logical consciousness, which says, of course, that's a dumb question. If there is hesitation, doubt or an outright no, ask the next question. What beliefs or thoughts have I accepted or created which hinder my healing? This can be the beginning of deep insight and attitudinal change. Your answer may be "I have tried but the disease is bigger than I am." Here lies the source of non-healing. For some reason you have empowered the disease rather than yourself. In these situations unresolved anger internalized with self-deprecation and dependency make disease large and you small. If you can turn this energy of anger into determination and conviction that you are capable of all self-healing you have taken the gigantic leap toward health. This new attitude will facilitate your concentration of energy on the body healing itself. It will make it possible for you to manipulate the electromagnetic field, to create self-healing rituals using sound, color and movement to change any negative beliefs and to make your energy field glowing and coherent.

Such deep work is not done in an instant, as you didn't get ill suddenly; this takes time. But ask yourself, would I rather invest the time and concentration in obtaining a complete cure and health or would I rather go the partial route to pay my money and have it done for me, not as well but at least enough to calm my symptoms? Your mind must make these decisions for your body.

## ACCESSING THE IMMUNE SYSTEM BY SCALAR ENERGY

*H*ealth is the ideal state of a constantly self-healing organism. Before disease or dysfunction settle into tissue the immune system, the body's first line of defense, with its protective hormones, enzymes and cells has become weakened. Yet regardless of the state of the immune system if the transportation of these vital substances to the tissue cells is blocked or inefficient the local tissue sickens. Sluggish, lymphatic circulation occurs when the body is unable to handle normal metabolic substances and particularly the tissue protein from viral, bacterial and cancer distruction.

We sense such circulatory disturbances with local tightness and pain and we learn to place heat or cold on the areas to make them feel better. Our hands gravitate to the tender spots to rub softly or dig deeply into the tightness. We know that massage, manipulation, rhythmic exercises and body work assist our rapid healing.

One doctor tells us that our immune system is not handling the problem and that we need drugs or shots to stimulate the weak system or extensive lab tests to find out the cause. Almost never do doctors try to evaluate the state of the lymphatic circulation as a primary or equal source of our body's poor immune response.

The exquisite specificity of the chemical aspects of the immune system seem to have helped doctors to forget that the important transportation of immunity may be lagging. To reiterate, our earlier statement that before disease or dysfunction takes place the immune systems guards have been overcome. Also the flexible plasticity of a healthy body is lost the result of disease or aging.

During my extensive research of hands-on-healers and psychic surgeons who effect deep tissue and open the body surfaces I pondered many questions. How was it possible to part skin, nerves, blood vessels and connective tissue to open deeper tissues without trauma? And how is it possible to re-suture such a spontaneous incision without a scar, pain or break in tissue integrity? I intuitively sensed that somehow the energy used by psychic surgeons was different from that generated by average good hands-on-healers. As a researcher of energy fields I was less interested in the psychic surgeons cure rates than in how they opened the body. Their explanation fell upon my deaf psychic ears.

One day I made a discovery. As my growing impressions came together, I realized that there was no electromagnetic wave action, that somehow opening the body was accomplished in a more passive state. Serendipitously I recalled the static scalar, standing wave, a concept in physics still in its infancy. Here is my brief review.

The energy that we experience in our bodies is electromagnetic waves radiating from the atoms of all our tissue cells. When this energy radiates away from the originating atoms it has a life of its own as an organized electromagnetic field now available to interact with other atoms and fields. If such electromagnetic waves meet head on at 180 degrees with another wave of the same frequency a scalar wave is created. This means that the energy from the two like waves does not take another direction or even a different frequency. Instead it becomes an enfolded, thicker glob of the same energy or a standing scalar field. At first this scalar energy was believed to be a vacuum. Now we know it is a dynamic pile of non directional energy. We have known that all fields have surface bonds which keep fields relatively intact and not dissipating. Yet when the surface bond is weakened the field expands in all directions, smoothly.

With this information in mind we experimented with creating the scalar wave inside the body by focused breathing (see instructions). We discovered that when we released the surface tension by thought the scalar expanded rapidly in all directions. The scalar energy became less dense and as such the cellular tissue followed the same path as it became less compressed. The lymphatic circulation was then under less pressure and flowed more freely. As a result the cellular protoplasm also dedensified making the tissue less turgid. People experienced that the painful tight areas of the body became lighter, thinner and less engorged. In such a softer state the body accelerated its healing by removing the tissue "garbage" and bathing the cells with the immune system "guards."

*53*

These concepts are among the most significant discoveries coming from my Bioenergy Fields Laboratory in the 28 years of its existence. This will be a major emphasis of our future research. Meantime, we have created meditation exercises for you to create and release the scalar energy.

I believe if you learn the following scalar exercises you will activate your self-healing of all illnesses faster than any other single exercise in this Mind Mastery Meditation book. Before you practice any specific meditation suggested to heal your disabilities you should first activate your scalar field.

# ❧ INSTRUCTIONS ❧
## CREATE A SCALAR WAVE

❖ Prepare your field by breathing through and spinning the chakras

❖ This exercise can be learned best by sitting practice. After acquiring the skill it can be repeated while standing and lying.

❖ Visualize your entire body as a container where you will draw in electromagnetic energy with with each inhalation. Unlike the breathing exercises to expand your field in chapter 2, page 10, this time you bring the energy into the center of your body. Do not move it out or up or down, just in.

❖ Start by breathing through the front of your body --- head to toe. When you have established this reflex, focus your attention upon breathing through the back of your body into the center where it contacts the "front energy" and folds upon itself going nowhere.

❖ Next breathe through both sides of your body simultaneously, right and left from head to toes. Let the energy again meet the same opposing energy building up and enfolding into a scalar standing field in the body center.

❖ Now concentrate upon the top of your head and the bottom of your feet to breathe in energy toward each other until it meets in the middle of the body to enfold upon itself. You have now created a powerful quiet quantity of energy in your bodily center.

54

❖ Now is when the quantity of energy begins expanding outward through all your cells toward the body surface. This is like an inflated balloon becoming larger --- or like a big glob of moist substance on a paper towel the energy is expanding outward on the surface beyond its original space. Allow this to continue until the center scalar energy has been dissipated outward loosening tight muscles and connective tissue and expanding the space between cells.

❖ Create the scalar field again but this time try to breathe from all directions into the center of the body simultaneously --- as though you are a radiating sun that is now reversing its energy inward on each inhalation to centralize the energy. If you have difficulty comprehending all sides at once go back to the first meditation with isolated directions.

❖ When your scalar field is full you will start to experience its spontaneous even expansion toward the body surfaces. You focus your attention upon allowing this slow spreading apart of all cells giving them "breathing room." The body area will seem larger and more resilient.

# ❦❧ SUGGESTIONS ❧❦

✿ Place your mind in a receptive intent to assist your scalar wave and to expand it. Avoid strong conscious intent which causes anti-coherence in the electromagnetic waves which limits the spontaneous creation of a non-directional pool of scalar energy.

✿ Focus your attention upon the general experience of removing the curbs, lowering the surface tension of the scalar energy to slowly expand.

✿ Note the sensory difference in formerly tense parts of your body and the warm flush which often occurs in the circulation.

✿ Later ask yourself if any of the pain or discomfort has gone.

✿ Repeat whenever you wish while lying or standing.

# ❦ INSTRUCTIONS ❧

## PREPARING THE FIELD FOR SELF-HEALING

✤ Repeat your preparation exercises by grounding yourself. Breathe through your chakras to increase your energy flow. Spin your chakras to expand your field frequencies.

✤ Bring forth an image of the healthiest and happiest time of your life. See yourself with vigorous, youthful health, glowing with enthusiasm for life and eagerness to overcome all obstacles. Firmly anchor that in your mind as you feel your body growing in strength and size with happy secure emotion.

✤ When this expanded state is firmly established turn on the "Rainbow Tape" sounds from The *Music of Light* tape set.* Take time for each of these procedures. If you find this tape comfortable you should play at least one 13-minute segment. If you find it too stimulating during the first self-healing meditations, turn off the sound and just sense your increasing body vibrations. Individuals' responses differ widely to this music. Most people have no difficulty with this tape; however, I do not want your field stimulated faster than you can comfortably integrate.

✤ Now allow yourself to drift upward and make contact with your "lovingness." This time experience the lovingness of yourself and the beautiful world. Don't hurry.

✤ Next ask to see and contact your highest spiritual image. A spiritual leader may come to take your hand; angels may surround you or Christ, Buddha, a wise man or God may appear.

*56*

✤ Allow this spiritual place to fuse with your feelings of lovingness. Experience the full complete and powerful physical, emotional and spiritual field which you are. Stay in that field which you are until it is well locked into your consciousness. Don't rush on until you are sure the preparation work is completed.

* Malibu Publishing Co., P.O. Box 4234, Malibu, CA, 90265, (310) 457-4694

# ❧ SUGGESTIONS ☙

✿ Remember your primary focus is upon breathing these sound vibrations through your entire field, rather than through your ears. This is done by focusing upon your entire field... the aura outside the body

✿ Stay with the image of your healthiest, happiest time by seeing many images of what you did when you had so much vitality. Take as long a time as these pleasant images appear. See Chapter 3, page 24. Happiness

✿ If clear images of lovingness come slowly, review Lovingness Meditations, Chapter 3, page 28.

✿ If your spiritual imagery is not clear and strong think of a time or place where you had a divine, mystical experience, or where you had words or colors that brought you a profound spiritual awareness.

✿ The effectiveness of the future healing meditations will be related to your success in these preparatory experiences. When you think you are ready for healing specific deficiencies ask the question, "Am I ready now to focus upon my health problems?" Await the answer from your highest consciousness. If the answer is yes, proceed to the next instructions. If the answer is no, continue to focus upon any aspect of your preparation which seems weak.

# INSTRUCTIONS

## HEALING HYPO-DEFICIENCY DISABILITIES

*D*eficiencies in the low frequency vibrations of the energy field are found in fatigue syndromes, endocrine deficiencies, low blood pressure, diabetes, cancer and poor lymphatic circulation.

✤ Visualize the warm color spectrum of red-orange and amber. Turn on the red-orange-amber auric sound tape from The *Music of Light* tape set, to bring abundant stimulation to your cells to carry out their natural work. Drums, rattles or percussive recordings with quick strong beats can be used.

✤ Breathe the sounds and colors through the entire body surface. This will stimulate simultaneously the gastrointestinal, cardiovascular and breathing systems. Later you can breathe specifically through your heart, lungs, intestines, genitals or skin, areas associated with your medical problem.

### Imagery: (choose one or several)

1. Visualize orange-red lava flowing down a hillside. You are a safe distance away. But the brilliance holds your vision glued to the image of lava as it slowly flows downward to the sea.

2. Visualize a sunset that is vividly rich in reds, oranges and deep colors. Sense that it carries tremendous strength. Breathe that energy into yourself and feel the stimulating effects.

3. Think of a specific situation which irritates you the most, i.e., being underestimated or taken advantage of, or a political or religious situation. Feel the anger rise but as soon as it is full blown, transfer the energy to your body and give up the frustrating angry situation.

4. Visualize a powerful, healthy, aggressive animal radiating his strength as king of the world; a lion and an elephant are particularly helpful. Observe that animal with a wide angle lens until you have lost sight of the animal but can experience his power in you --- your energy, your limbs and your intent. Visualize this energy in small swirls of energy across your upper chest out to your axilla and from your pubic bone out to the pelvic rims of your hip bones. These are areas of the lymphatic nodes that are congested. You can also use your finger tips in a small circular massage. Think of hormones and T-cells flooding your lymphatic system.

# ❧ SUGGESTIONS ☙

✿ Because these exercises are strong stimulants your breathing and heart rate should increase. This is desirable. If you become uncomfortably stimulated stop the exercise. These operate like an exercise which one must build up to.

✿ You will come to learn from these exercises that repressed or forgotten emotions, aggression and anger also repress the body's physiology. The nature of your deficiency disease stems from unconsciously slowing down of the dynamic life force, whereas the specific classification or location of the disease is determined more by genetics and lifestyle.

✿ Deep imagery often brings spectacular changes in sensory experiences such as feeling hot or cold, tingling, itching, losing sensation, or feeling heaviness in certain areas of the body. These occur because of your energy field changes. Because we have no specific nerve endings to record field changes all sensory nerves may respond to field changes giving us bizarre combinations of information. Therefore, there are no universal sensory descriptions associated with healing imagery.

✿ Earlier writings describing meditations for cancer placed too much angry emphasis on killing or hating the disease. These meditations followed the old allopathic model that described cutting it out, destroying it chemically or overshadowing it by a battle of the good against the bad. Such an attitude toward cancer seems wrong to me because too often hate of cancer becomes hate of self, further depressing the body's physiology.

✿ A much sounder approach considers the cancer as a temporary, undesirable condition while the mind recognizes the power of the self to activate the body's healing response.

*59*

# INSTRUCTIONS

## HEALING HYPERACTIVE DISEASES

*H*yperactivity of the physiological systems result in major diseases such as hypertension, high blood pressure, chronic inflammation, arthritis, hyperthyroidism, allergies, skin rashes, colitis and tachicardia. In all of these conditions we find the energy field overflowing with the lower red-orange vibrations and undernourished with the higher blue-violet frequencies.

Quiet elevating meditations help to calm all of these diseases because as the frequency of the field goes up the body's physiology slows down.

✣ Prepare your field with the relaxation and chakra exercises.

### Imagery: (choose one or several)

1. Visualize your field inside and out in a soft blue light like the sky on a peaceful summer day. Play the blue, violet and mauve relaxing tape from The *Music of Light* tape set or play soft lullabies. Breathe the color and sound vibrations into all areas of your body. Concentrate breathing through your legs, arms and lastly through the large bodily cavities. Later you may want to breathe these soothing energies through a local area where there is pain or more involvement. Experience the entire body with the same expansive softness.

2. Visualize the myriad of stars in a warm summer sky, twinkling in slow pulsing rhythms. Get lost in that image. Occasionally remind yourself that this tranquillity is happening in your body.

**60**

3. Visualize sparkling blue water, the ocean or a large lake where you can see beyond into infinity. You are in a secure craft drifting and dreaming in a warm late afternoon sun. The lap of the water against your boat is like a lullaby.

4. Visualize yourself floating on a fluffy cloud cradled by a moon beam and allow your body to become a part of this picture.

5. Visualize your body like a river that has come tumbling out of the mountains down a tumultuous path now reaching the tranquillity of the alluvial plains. Tributaries are branching everywhere (like your capillaries) filling slowly with water and lowering the river's pressure and speed. See the river bed expanding slowly and being lost in the land. Feel the softness occurring in your tissue; as you internalize the expanding river flow you feel your blood vessels dilating, your pulse and pressure becoming slower and steady. Sense your happy body as you languish in this state.

# ❧ SUGGESTIONS ❧

✿ By preparing the field and performing the visualizations I offer, you can later create your own images that are more related to your experiences.

✿ After practicing these exercises your automatic reflexes will change. If practiced, these perceptual processes of imagery and sensitivity will help reprogram your thoughts, your field and the physiology of your disease.

✿ Sometime later check your blood pressure --- not immediately --- because the intent is not to lower blood pressure but to expand the field. The secondary result over time will be the lower blood pressure.

✿ Occasionally throughout the day remember the expanded river image for a few moments to keep the feedback loop strong.

# ❦⊙INSTRUCTIONS⊙❦

## Healing Neuromuscular Injuries And Fractures

*I*f your medical problem is swelling and congestion from virus colds, fractures or sprains follow the general procedures for preparing the field.

✤ Use the river bed expansion visualization (on page 60) for a short time only --- not over 5 or 10 minutes. Follow by breathing in and out through the area of congestion while at the same time visualizing healing blue energy bathing injured areas as you inhale. Play the blue, violet, mauve music tape (from The *Music of Light* tape set). Note that the color of your breath has changed to a darker red or purple as you exhale. You are removing the excess inflammatory frequencies from your field. Continue the "blue" vibrations frequently for 72 hours on bad sprains, dislocations or fractures and swelling.

## Visualizations

✤ Visualize the red imagery (see page number 58 with your blood vessels dilating to allow healing blood to flow to and from the swollen area.

✤ With fractures or major limb trauma, visualize your red blood cells as bright red dump trucks. At the chest area as you breathe in you fill the dump trucks full of oxygen and nutrients and as you exhale you send them hustling out your blood vessels to the injured areas. There your red blood cell trucks dump their healing substances.

**62**

✤ These busy little trucks don't return to the lung empty handed. Contrariwise, on inspiration they again fill, this time with the waste products of injury and swelling to hasten to the lungs for disposal through the lungs and kidneys. According to our research this exercise will shorten the recovery period by weeks or even months.

✤ When the swelling and pain are decreased change the images from blue-violet images to red-orange ones, to increase the circulation and regenerate new cells.

✿ Dense tissue like bones, cartilage and ligaments has a slower moving, lower frequency field and will take longer to heal than nerves or glands which have more pliable tissue and a faster more dynamic field. Removing pain and swelling caused by muscle injury of the field is fast. But the actual repair of damaged dense tissue, tendons, ligaments, bones and cartilage or healing the destructive changes from arthritis can take considerably longer.

✿ Degenerated tissue with nerve and muscle loss are the slowest in healing and without activating the field, they may never regenerate. Remember however, that your field holds the template, the pattern for regeneration and you have within your body the cells which regenerate nerve, bone and endocrine tissue. These new cells can be captured and organized into new tissue.

63

# ❧❦INSTRUCTIONS❦❧

## HEALING NEUROSENSORY DISTURBANCES AND DEGENERATION

✤   With neurosensory disturbances such as deafness, visual and sensory loss or muscular weakness, complete all field preparatory exercises (see page no. 56).

✤   Visualize the location of the disturbance and breathe in and out with the field in these colors.  Use the yellow, green and gold tape from The *Music of Light* tape set. Visualize a net like structure with innumerable communication circuits like a giant switchboard inside the disturbed area.  Notice that only a few circuits are lighted. Imagine that you have brought in a great surge of energy to fill those circuits. Gradually all tracks light up like an electric dimmer that has been turned brighter.

✤   If you experience a circuit overload back off for a few minutes to allow your nerves to reach a peak carrying capacity.  Now you can see the area as a busy, functioning but not overloaded, system.  You will see the area becoming brighter until you feel the nerves buzzing with aliveness.  Continue to use the yellow, green and gold sounds.

✤   With paralyzed degenerated neuromuscular systems, visualize the area in full action.  If the problem is in the legs, visualize jogging or dancing with full flowing action.  If in the arms, visualize an active sport using that limb or again using the arms to communicate in dancing or mime.  Imaging large movements is essential. Turn off and on with the red, orange and amber sound tapes.

*64*

# ❧ SUGGESTIONS ❧

✿   Neuromuscular disturbances can have many sources but changing the field is essential to healing all of these.  From injury, shock and surgery the nerves may forget how to operate in a coordinated manner.  The injury may have caused a shutdown of the synapses --- the connections between nerves --- so that the nerve impulses are short-circuited.  Play the yellow, green and gold tape from The *Music of Light* tape set  because these have the same frequencies as the synapses.  Give them a jump charge.  Sensory defects, hearing and visual loss may improve immediately when the circuit is reconnected.

✿   To regenerate lost muscle or nervous tissue also play the red, orange and amber sound tape.

65

# INSTRUCTIONS

## HEALING BARRIER DISEASES

This is not a medical classification but an energy field description of a group of diseases such as scleroderma, psoriasis, multiple sclerosis and Lou Gerhig's disease. Persons with these disabilities have a pronounced functional energy field pattern. Their field is rigid to electromagnetic energy flowing in and out of their bodies. Laboratory recordings of the energy field show that it does not respond to a hands-on healer's energy, to light, sound or electrically- generated frequencies. It is a field that is very protected by an emotional barrier to energy field transactions. It is as though the body is wrapped in an impenetrable cocoon, isolated as an island with unscaleable cliffs. There is first an energy field barrier that must be weakened. Although all healing is possible these barrier diseases require major emotional release and reorganization which generally requires the assistance of a trained counselor. But the pattern of the barrier must also be removed from the field.

✤ Repete meditations to Prepare The Field For Self Healing page 56, and Healing Neurosensory Disturbances page 64 and Healing Neuromuscular Injuries page 62.

✤ Practice regularly creating and expanding the Scalar Resting Wave page 54.

# ❦ⓒ SUGGESTIONS ⓢ❦

✿ If any of your health conditions are acute, be gentle. You will play the tapes for a shorter time. Breathe in and out less forcefully. Soften the colors from a strong blue or red or yellow to a pastel shade. Turn the sounds down low. Gently move the red dump trucks in a smooth pattern. Recognize that your body needs time to reorganize its field that has been perhaps many years structured in this destructive way. Your body must relearn how to use this energy to reorganize itself. As a self-healer you are your own coach to hasten your body's own healing response.

✿ Practice your selected mediations at least twice a day for at least 30 minutes each. Remember to go through the entire sequence each time - preparation, specific exercises and imagery. The preparation will take less time as you establish a routine so that more time is available for the holistic healing. Establish a habit of self-healing meditation like your routine of bathing and brushing your teeth.

✿ Close each session by gradually changing the focus of your consciousness to everyday reality. Survey your entire energy field vibrations and physical sensations. Recognize and acknowledge when changes in pain and symptoms take place.

✿ Survey your emotional state and the power you experience when you know you are in command and what you envision can happen. Know that you have given your body the most powerful stimulus to heal itself --- the power of your mind.

✿ May I remind you that you can improve any tissue since all cells and molecules are replaced constantly throughout life, some faster than others. These replacements should be with new and healthy cells. Unfortunately these are generally replaced by the same type of sick cells that existed unless you change the pattern that has been anchored in the field.

*67*

✿ Give thanks for this divine healing capacity which you have experienced and used. Know that this skill becomes progressively more available to heal you, to refine your senses and behaviors and to enrich your life. Many cherish the opportunities they find during their illness.

# ASSISTING IN ANOTHER'S HEALING

$\mathcal{W}$e all have the capacity to heal ourselves and others. Some of us do it spontaneously without instruction. Others want formal classes. Of the many excellent teachers, I recommend Rosalind Bruyere and Barbara Brennan as outstanding. But wherever you go your energy goes with you, actually preceding your body. If you go to see an ill or recovering person intend to take your healthiest and most radiant field. Remember that with you in your mind-field, you also bring your concerns and problems and confusions. Ill people are particularly sensitive to the emotional states of their guests. Of all the gifts you could take the person, not flowers and sweets or books but your healing vibrations will have the most lasting effects. Before you enter the hospital stabilize and enliven your field.

Remember despite your deep concerns for this person's recovery be sure to fill your field with lovingness and coherent energy that will radiate from you to fill the room. Don't stay a long time, just long enough to implant your coherent loving energy. If you make physical contact with the person expand and lighten your field to be available for the sick one to use to clarify his. Remember you don't need to be a trained healer nor do you need to purposefully "channel" energy to them. Your intent to bring your coherent loving energy to them is more than adequate.

# REMOVING ANESTHESIA

$\mathcal{G}$eneral anesthesia when given by inhalation or injection is a foreign poisonous substance stored in tissue. It takes some time to dissipate via regular fluid circulation. Anesthesia leaves rational consciousness within hours yet it may take days or weeks to leave the body. Worse yet, some of the anesthetic may remain forever cloistered in the cells.

Actually it is the field which permeates all tissue that initially holds the anesthesia. The essence of the anesthetic lodges in the abdomen where circulation is the poorest. The body's natural healing does not start until this toxic substance is removed. This accounts for long recovery periods after surgery.

When anesthesia is removed, tissue healing begins immediately and rapidly. Experienced healers quickly and safely remove anesthetic from patients by alluring the toxic field to the body's surface then attracting it to the field of their hands to remove it.

If you are the one anesthetized, when you return to consciousness first focus your attention on your abdomen. Breathe deeply into your abdomen by expanding your stomach on inhalation and exhale completely out your nose, being aware that you are mixing the anesthetic field with the air that you discharge. If you get dizzy take smaller breaths or repeat one of the grounding exercises (see page no. 10), before you return to the decontamination breathing. Depending on your ability to concentrate, this procedure may take place on and off for several hours. Make every effort to slowly breathe out this toxic field. It is the most important and primary self-healing event. Continue this deep abdominal breathing daily for several days.

Many experienced healers have asked me to share in more detail my techniques for removing anesthetic from another person immediately after surgery. Even novice healers can carry out these simple procedures. Persons with no experience with hands-on healing can also perform this miracle with a little instruction. Don't be apprehensive; it cannot harm either of you. To become acquainted with the energy field practice on yourself. Hold your two hands, palms facing several inches apart. Allow the field of each hand to make contact with the other. Your focus will be on the subtle feelings in your hands. Otherwise, you are not consciously involved. After four or five minutes gradually try to move your hands farther apart. Note the pull or attraction of your two hands. Play with this sensation by moving your hands closer and farther apart until you reach a distance where the field bonds seem to be broken. This is the sensation you will now feel as you hold your hand over the abdomen of an anesthetized person. You will feel the net between you and a suction of attraction between your fields. This time the ill person's field may sting your hand or feel prickly and in turmoil. These are accurate sensations for the confused and hyperactive field of the anesthetized patient.

With your hand held a few inches above the abdomen start a slow movement upward and away from his body pulling that energy bond with you until at some distance it becomes so weak you no longer sense it...To be more effective at the same time that you pull the anesthetic field upward you can create a greater suction by breathing in through your hand and drawing the anesthetic field into your lower arm. When you exhale move the anesthetized energy out your elbow so that it does not enter deeply into your main body field. When I first discovered this way of removing anesthesia I brought the breath through my body and out my nose. Needless to say, I learned as I became anesthetized and the patient became alert. I erred in not discharging the incoming breath through the elbow. Using this technique your lower arm may have some temporary sensory disturbance but your field does not basically change. A few breaths in and out through your hand after you have finished with the patient will remove your sensory disturbance. After ten to twenty minutes the patient will become aware of his surroundings; color will return to his face as circulation improves and breathing deepens. Others in the room may smell a strong odor as the anesthetic dissipates in the atmosphere.

69

# ☙ INSTRUCTIONS ❧

## SELF-HEALING RITUALS

Create your own self-healing imagery from which you expand into a self-healing ritual.

✤ Choose a setting for your ritual, perhaps a location such as India, Egypt, Greece, South America or a pastoral or native environment, or an imposing structure or temple you have seen. If you wish, create your own healing space but give it reality with structures, colors, sounds and ambiance.

✤ Bring into this setting the people or animals you wish to assist you with their presence. These should be living beings that you love, admire or will energize your field.

✤ Review the suggested colors for disease classifications and give your setting a color spectrum that suits your energy needs. You will have a wide range of shades and hues within each color spectrum.

✤ Choose appropriate sounds or rhythms for your ritual that serve your energy field needs.

✤ Use inner symbols which have deep meaning for you to create spiritual ceremonies of initiation or celebration. You may also draw on nature and the cosmos for your rituals. Make yourself the leading character. Become a warrior, a priest, a regal male or female, a wise one, a teacher or a healer.

✤ Check to see that each choice you have made to compose your ritual has deep emotional meaning for you. Your concentrated pure emotions must be involved to truly focus all of these energy sources for your healing.

✤ Bring in observers or a watch dog if you wish --- a silent partner to acknowledge and witness your work.

# SUGGESTIONS

✿ As you visualize the setting for your healing ritual observe the many parts of the image so it becomes firmly anchored in your mind.

✿ When you start, bring in only a few people and animals to increase your primary purpose which is to heal yourself.

✿ For this exercise you may select the color blends and combinations which you like and the sounds that are compatible with the entire scene,

✿ An observer or watch dog is important only to provide emotional comfort for you.

## SELF-HELP NUTRITION

$\mathcal{N}$o matter how carefully you select your diet, each day's food is in some way nutritionally deficient. With the masses of people to be fed from our land we have overfarmed our soil creating deficiencies, particularly in minerals. There is ample evidence that our water which resupplies the soil with minerals is grossly lacking in minerals. Thus our vegetables cannot store adequate minerals or build vitamins for supplying nutrition for our domesticated animals or for our own needs. Certainly, products rushed to markets great distances from the farms require harvesting before they reach peak nutritional value. Understandably we are mineral and vitamin deficient.

Aggressive popular advertising from the multimillion dollar supplement business has convinced us of our needs. Self-help nutritional books are best sellers. Yet we generally follow the new fads applied to special segments of our population: athletes, pregnant women, or those of want to lose weight and gain the "beautiful body." Unfortunately few people have the background to evaluate the extensive but questionable nutritional research used to convince us. We tend to follow the recommended daily requirements for vitamins and minerals that were established years ago and are not adequate for today's pace. Also, the expanded consciousness of individuals today requires more minerals to maintain the higher tone of the nervous system and the stable ionization of the energy field to maintain tissue absorption. When I view the nutritional dilemma from the point of view of a physiological researcher who has studied nutrition for fifty years, there are basic issues that each of us must solve for ourselves. (1) How much of which basic foods should I eat, and (2) how do I know that I get the proper amount of vitamins and minerals for my specific needs?

72

First, if you have major medical and health problems I encourage you to seek a well-trained nutritional counselor to assist you and your physician. Unless they have advanced recent training in nutrition, most physicians are not prepared to supervise a healthful diet. Medical schools at best, provide one nutrition course and generally only a few lectures to medical students.

Because this is a book on self-healing in which I recommend individual healing programs I must also recommend an approach to the planning of your overall food consumption and an individuaal mineral and vitamin approach which targets health.

The criteria for the appropriate proportion of fats, carbohydrates and proteins, the building blocks of life, now in use were established earlier in this century. These gravely need further research, study and revision. It is understandable why so many new approaches spring up based upon disease deficiencies and the needs of particular groups, such as the athletes, the fatigued, and the aging.

What do we know in general about these nutritional building blocks? A high carbohydrate diet provides heat and quick energy that is more important in some climates and with some ways of life; it causes weight gain; it is necessary to repair and replace cells. A high fat diet very efficiently supplies energy over an extended time --- longer than carbohydrates; it creates fatty acids that optimize body functions but also tend to clog blood vessels and to cause weight gain.

When we consider selecting vitamins and minerals the story becomes even more complex. Many supplements contain undesirable fillers such as corn, wheat and sugar which stimulate allergic responses with overuse. Combining separate minerals and vitamins in a convenient one a day pill is not sound scientifically and certainly is geared only to mass consumers. It is a shot in the dark approach. Currently popular mineral supplements are created with the attitude that the more the merrier, with as many as 72 separate minerals, many of which have never been found in the body. Those that have, are not dosed in proportion to the constituents of human blood.

I believe strongly that we should have the knowledge and the opportunity to choose specifically what our body needs at the time. I recommend *The Zone; A Dietary Road Map by Barry Sears, Harper Collins Books, N.Y., 1995*, a book which makes an important contribution by exploding the myth that we should all be vegetarians with a fat-free diet. Barry Sears, a qualified biomedical researcher formerly on staff at M.I.T. cites important, even "Noble Prize" winning research that has been published in major research journals but not recognized in the field of nutrition. He offers exciting new information about the essential proportions of carbohydrates, proteins and fats. He includes workbook exercises for understanding the quantities of these substances to include in your diet based on your sex, age and lifestyles, etc.

For the most advanced information about minerals I refer you to the popular book by *Lendon Smith, Feed Your Body Right (M. Evans & Co., N.Y., 1994)* and my book **Infinite Mind:** *Science of the Human Vibrations of Consciousness*, pages 270-274. Smith wrote his book to explain the nutritional supplement program of "Life Balances" by John Kitkoski in Spokane, Washington. This program provides an essential missing link to our prior discussion of minerals, stressing the pH or alkaline - acid balance in healthy cellular activity. Kitkoski, a visionary biochemist with years of significant research with animals and humans, has discovered that when the acid-alkaline balance is disturbed, neither the blood nor the cells can absorb the vitamins and minerals regardless of the foods or supplement ingested.

*73*

Unless there is a negative ion charged acidity in the intestine and blood the minerals do not cross the membranes to the blood and eventually into cells. So the problem is not just what you eat or which supplement you take but the condition of the body to absorb these. You can be vitamin and mineral deficient in the cells even with a dietary overabundance. With age, for some even a young age, the exchange of minerals and nutrients at the cellular level becomes inefficient. The metabolic wastes accumulate in the tissue, creating a toxic condition of cells and systems --- the destructive beginning of disease.

Kitkoski's* recommendations for dosage of his ionized minerals (in liquid pH active forms) is based upon the normal proportion of minerals in the blood to carry out their unique functions. Specifically, he creates a personalized program based on your particular blood deficiencies on the ideal ratio of companion minerals. Your mineral program may be changed when blood tests show improvement. Keep in mind that mineral pills are not ionized and thus do not contain the electrical activity --- pH plus and minus charges which insure mineral absorption. Most mineral pills cannot be used by the body.

*Life Balances, Inc., P.O.Box 28921, Spokane, WA, 99228, (509) 455-9976

The "Life Balances" program supplies only pure vitamins not mixtures and those which the body needs. But even more exciting it provides a way for you to know which vitamins you need each day --- you become the knowledgeable judge. The "Life Balances" program provides a kit of twenty vitamins in individual containers. Each day you smell the contents of each vitamin container separately. These will have a pleasant odor, no odor, or a bad odor based on your nutritional condition. Those that smell bad, you don't need. Those that smell good you do need and those that smell slightly pleasant or neutral you need less. Because your nutritional needs are based upon your work, play, emotions and health conditions as well as the food you eat, your vitamin and mineral needs will also change. How great that at last "Life Balances" has given us a way to discover and supply our nutritional needs without overdosing, wasting money or ending up depleted. I have chosen the Kitkoski program for myself for a number of years because it works for me and others.*

74

•Dr. Hunt has no financial interest in the Life Balances Company.

# ❧ SUMMARY & CONCLUSIONS ☙

$\mathcal{B}$riefly at the beginning of this chapter I commented that healing is our immediate goal and health our ultimate one. Both goals are better accomplished when the individual takes over command of his own life and health, while building a healthy attitude toward his body and a determined vigilance over his lifestyle choices.

With intent I did not include the shaman healing practices of evoking animal power or spiritual allies from whom knowledge is supposedly gained and power manipulated. I believe these are artificial ways to empower a person in order to initiate the healing response but these are not permanent. Such practices do not insure that the individual gains a greater capacity to command and direct his energy field to alter his body's response to disturbing situations and to continuously heal himself. Only by deep involvement of the mind-field are these goals accomplished.

In all my writing and lectures I have rejected the shamanic belief that illness results from entities invading the body from without or that disease is punishment for unacceptable behavior. Treatment in these instances must destroy, exorcise or protect against such invasions by counter demonic or purifying rituals. In a similar vein are the beliefs that the dark side of magic can place a hex or punish the person for misdeeds ending in death or disease.

Let me summarize by saying that the human energy field is affected by conditions of the environment before we breathe in pure or contaminated air or before we ingest nourishing or poisonous substances. Therefore, the human field is the first line of defense against disease and the pervading condition of our field is the ultimate indication of our health.

In this chapter I have presented tried and true exercises to hasten your body's healing response, to make your human field more coherent, strong and perfect, and to assist in your evolution as a person through Mind Mastery.

76

# Chapter 6
#  DISCOVERING SPIRITUALITY

Without doubt a belief in some form of deity occurred in all cultures which developed art, rituals and group behaviors. The idea of God, extended consciousness beyond basic survival demands to allow a level of transcendence. The mystical realm became a fact in man's life. The Mind Mastery concepts stress the importance of accessing all levels of consciousness that are available to humans. When he touches the highest level of thought, spirituality follows hand in hand. Here he reaches into the vibratory space where he comprehends universal thought, knowledge and wisdom.

The skills for Mind Mastery are potentially available to all humans even if they are not readily accessible to many. Religious beliefs often provide the greatest barriers to attaining these skills. Religion sprang from man's experience with "one God" and became anchored by the teachings of the Bible, the Koran, and the Buddhist scriptures.

From common beginnings man developed various doctrines and tenants to guide his behaviors and beliefs. These resulted in formalized religion. In turn, religion gained authority by tapping into human thought and intellectually molding individuals minds. A universal intellectual understanding of God was emphasized, making God a remote being who remained forever illusive. Most people experienced God in the same way. Yet throughout the history of religion there were visionaries who had had profound emotional encounters with God. Their stories of their encounters rallied others with similar experiences to redirect their beliefs toward a mystical and highly personal God. This idea of a personal God weakened religious authority and led to a heightened spirituality. Sensory information came from higher states of consciousness to transform the experience from a rational one to a mystical illumination; consciousness was therefore extended.

The fundamental difference between thinking about spirituality and experiencing it became clear. Unless thought activates human emotions, thought is powerless --- it remains a mere intellectual construct. Herein lies the major difference between religion and spirituality. Religion is often logical and comfortable; spirituality may be emotional and frightening.

Spirituality is marked by mystical experience charged with great emotion; religious beliefs are transformed from an impersonal believing to a personal knowing. The experience of God will differ from person to person. Because we experience God not objectively but mystically, it is impossible to know Him in the way that others do. The basis of spirituality is not to be found in the physical nature of the universe but rather in the spiritual, mystical experiences of humans.

The mystical approach to spirituality is an ancient if not universal one. Early records show elaborate testimonies by Jews, Moslems and Christians who had sudden profound religious experiences. Mystics wrote books demonstrating that by concentrating their awareness they could have real divine and personal experiences with God. The

Sufi Muslim sect proctored postures, movement, music and dancing to achieve a mystical state while encouraging inner awareness. We Westerners know them as the "Whirling Dervishes."

Theologians of the fourth century developed breathing exercises with concomitant body postures to focus their energy inward. Jewish mysticism was reported in the Kabala. Spanish mystical schools reported in *The Book Splendors* suggested methods to penetrate the inner life of God and human consciousness. Actually, the mystical teachings of all of the monotheistic religions represented a stage in human consciousness where the mystic ascends to God by descending into his own mind. God and man were considered inseparable. When the mystic acquired an understanding of his own deepest self he became aware of God's presence within him.

Not only religious leaders but many thinkers of the day held strong beliefs about God and mysticism. Plato and Spinoza believed that spontaneous intuitive knowledge revealed the presence of God while Descartes and Newton had no time for mystery. They explained God in rational, intellectual terms. Albert Einstein believed that mysticism was the source of all true art and science.

The recent flowering of Buddhism and Yoga in the United States has advanced the mystical aspects of spirituality. Joseph Campbell's formerly popular television program showing the universality of mystical consciousness and belief systems in dissimilar cultures has added fuel to the growing trend acknowledging mysticism as a fact ignored by the external trappings of religion.

I acknowledge some of the often enumerated problems of mysticism in religion. It is frequently said that the mystical God is not an objective reality but a profoundly subjective experience that leads to the abandonment of reason. Mysticism has been viewed as simply imagination. Actually, mysticism is not in conflict with reality but is an extension of reality into non-material dimensions. Objective reality does not exclude the transcendent reality of spiritual experiences. As a matter of fact, the concept of God itself is a prime example of a non-material reality which has continued to inspire people for thousands of years.

The literature abounds with warnings about the dangers of entering altered states in search of spiritual insights. Some otherwise enlightened clergy and psychiatrists liken higher states of consciousness to trips into darkness where the soul can be taken over by demons or where schizophrenia awaits the unprotected. This advice should be cautiously evaluated. Often these comments come from those who have never had a mystical experience. Some speak from fear of their own potential spiritual power. Others may be influenced by religious zealots with explosive religious fervor. These individuals are often ungrounded in earthy reality and undisciplined by a critical intellect.

Of course entering higher divine states of consciousness without instruction can lead to difficulty. Everyday perceptions are altered. This experience would be akin to finding oneself alone in a real space ship launched from the earth without instructions on how to cope with weightlessness or control the vehicle. We who are ordained as spiritual leaders who have experienced extended consciousness, know that the warnings are exaggerated. A step by step extension of consciousness into the mystical realm is imperative and has been successfully accomplished by many instructional systems. Long term meditators generally have these skills. However, because of the potential problems connected with spiritual states, this chapter is the last of a group directed toward developing internal consciousness. If you have practiced and become skilled in the exercises in the previous chapters, then you should have sufficient Mind Mastery to move comfortably and successfully into these final spiritual insights. The following meditations focus on releasing and integrating the great emotional life force, the biological level of consciousness, as it moves through the rational, intellectual level into the divine mystical plane, all without breaks in consciousness. Spirituality, then is experienced not as a traumatic isolated episode but as the culmination of continuously accessing levels of reality simutaneously without schisms. Then divinity and humanity are not different aspects of life, but rather they are extensions of consciousness along the continuum of reality. Both are profound.

One last clarification is in order. Unfortunately, some writers, even mystical leaders, speak about the importance of diminishing the personality and the ego in order to recognize the divine self. This is an outmoded concept. I know so very well that unless the personality-ego contact is maintained at all times, these divine characteristics never become a part of the everyday life and behavior of the individual.

# ❧ INSTRUCTIONS ☙

## PREPARING FOR MYSTICAL EXPERIENCES

*P*robably you are already acquainted with some of the startling sensory experiences that accompany perceptual awakenings. I enumerate these so that you will not be surprised:

✤ You may see a blinding white light beyond anything you have ever seen. This may take the form of stars, the sun, bursting Aurora Borealis, or halos around everything.

✤ You may experience increased spontaneous physical energy that can create energy waves. bodily jerks, and shakes or undulating movements.

✤ You may experience increased sensory awareness of heat or cold, sounds, and strong tastes and odors. The body image is often heightened or absent altogether. A rise of the "Kundalini serpent energy" up the spine is not unusual.

✤ Information and instruction in verbal or printed form may accompany divine "states." This information is like a charge. You receive information about your destiny and instructions to trust your divine guidance. This instruction is never concerned with the material world and everyday problems.

✤ A sense of oneness with the divine vibrations of the world can burst forth during which you feel no separation, where all is all and everything is perfect.

✤ For additional suggestions, review the chapter three, "Opening Emotions"

## PREPARING THE FIELD

*80*

✤ Repeat your preparation exercises by grounding yourself and breathing through your chakras.

✤ Remember several of your most satisfying accomplishments. Hear people praising your attainments. Feel your pride and self-worth growing. See a substantial physical image of yourself. Firmly anchor these images in your mind knowing that this is you at a deep level. Feel joy and release. Take time to remember this complete elaborate picture.

✤ When you have a clear image in your mind turn on the blue, violet and mauve tape from the *Music of Light* tape set. If these are not available, play your favorite peaceful classical music. These selections have a fuller spectrum of frequencies than most other quiet music.

✤ Allow your consciousness to drift upward as you recall your lovingness and thankfulness for your readiness for deeper spiritual experiences.

# SUGGESTIONS

❧ These preparation exercises may take several days. Each day should feel more comfortable. Continue these images until you have the urge to move on.

❧ You will notice that events in your daily routine are brighter and more pleasant. You experience fewer irritations.

❧ Follow your expanding imagery without trying to give the images linear rational meanings.

❧ If you should image a barrier, recall the suggestions in Chapter three on opening emotions.

❧ If a part of your self-worth which is less than divine comes to consciousness, let it slip away. Such images are not appropriate for your spiritual work. Don't repress them; rather, watch them disappear.

# ❦❧ INSTRUCTIONS ❦❧
## IMAGINING YOUR SPIRITUAL PATH

✤ See yourself walking down a path in a meadow toward a lazy meandering shallow stream. When you come to the stream you see that the water is clear and the bottom smooth and sandy, inviting you to go wading. Walk slowly up the stream being aware of the cool water against your bare feet and legs. Your movements in and out of the water make your feet tingle. Each time you pick up a foot you are aware of its aliveness. How is it different from everyday walking with your shoes on? You feel the bottoms of your feet being massaged by the shifting sand. Energy rushes upward making your legs strong and spry.

✤ Walk as long as you wish until your feet and legs feel a part of both the water and the land. You may substitute wading in a gentle surf at the sea shore.

✤ Cast your gaze forward to where the stream widens into a small pond or lake. Pause and look into the water to see your image. You will see a pleasant image of someone with high qualities. Ask if this image has something to tell you. Accept this person's characteristics as your own as you continue walking. They will expand and strengthen your self-image.

✤ If the image happens to be unpleasant don't evade it and don't incorporate it into your self-image. However, ask the image what it is trying to tell you. Remember, this mystical image is indicating some barriers to your moving ahead. Recognize that you may need to repeat some exercises in Chapter III, Opening Emotions. Take the time and don't be discouraged. We rarely eliminate all blocks the first time around. But never accept these unpleasant images as more than the memory of some unpleasant emotional experiences that you have not yet completely resolved.

✤ When you are ready, continue up the stream to the other end of the pond or lake. You notice that the stream comes from an incline where the water flows faster as it spills over rocks. You may feel more comfortable walking beside the stream. Follow the stream upward where tumbling waterfalls radiate more energy. Again monitor your imagery. Your grounded imagery will remain the same as will your mystical imagery of the water. But now with the increased energy from the tumbling water your entire field will brighten and with it may come bolder imagery.

# ❧ SUGGESTIONS ❧

✿ During the repetitive movement of walking, pay careful attention to your random, spontaneous imagery. Simple repetitive movements, like wading, tend to free emotional barriers that you may have built up.

✿ Continue this transitional exercise for several days if you wish or until you have the urge to move on.

✿ Remember you are submitting yourself to control and instruction from your higher self.

# ❦❦ INSTRUCTIONS ❦❦
## FOLLOWING THE LIGHT

✤ Turn on the "Relaxation Tape" from the *Music of Light* tape set. Breathe the color sounds of blue, violet and mauve through your entire body not just through your nose.

✤ When you are ready a light will appear at the horizon or higher in the sky. You will follow this new focus as you move away from the stream.

✤ Let your mind see dimensions of the light such as color, shapes and its source. As you move closer you will pass into a more enclosed pathway, like a trellis, an arbor, trees in rows or columns lining the path. Let your imagination describe your pathway to the light.

✤ As you approach a tunnel, the light may become a specific beam rather than being observed as a general brightness.

✤ If you have apprehension when you come to the tunnel entrance, stop for a moment to remember that the tunnel symbolizes a transition into a higher consciousness, one that you may have felt before as an altered state disconnected from day-to-day consciousness. With the preparation you have had in mastering your mind, consciousness is no longer broken into disparate segments. You should therefore move toward the end of the tunnel and the light.

✤ As you move toward the radiance see how close you can come to it. Allow it to encircle you, to engulf you and be a part of you.

*84*   ✤ Move into the light allowing your imagination to again expand into some grand imagery. Don't hurry to totally understand but check to see if you are grounded, expanded and fully conscious on all levels. Allow elaborate imagery to instruct you at the highest level. Now you are integrating three formerly subjected levels of consciousness.

# ❧ SUGGESTIONS ❧

❧ Generally, meditators are so enlivened when they approach a transcendent consciousness that they will get all the rational answers, put it all together, and be one with life. Remember, you are changing your capacity to extend your reality and the skill and security is more important than logical answers or the speed of your trip.

❧ We know that when people cross over into physical death, many transition via a tunnel with a light at the end. Apparently those of you who have already expanded your consciousness via the tunnel can move rapidly into the light without tunnels. The tunnel is characteristic of a change in consciousness. It does not herald death of the physical body.

❧ Some meditators find the light in the sky and wish to drift and live in that light forever, in limbo so to speak. Like spirituality, light must shine from your field at all times not just when you escape from the more mundane levels of consciousness. You must experience that light within yourself and know it is a part of you always.

# INSTRUCTIONS
## EXPERIENCING THE DIVINE LIGHT

✤ If you have ever had a divine light experience ask to see it again. Take time even if your imagery is blank for some time. Some people find a powerful light symbol like a sun that is overwhelmingly brilliant.

✤ If a person appears, approach him, observe his countenance, attitude and appearance. Ask him who he is and what he has come to tell you. You may be surprised at the answer you receive but know your highest self is making a new connection in your consciousness. Follow your imagery and experiences.

✤ When you have completed this episode recall your imagery and your sense of awe. If emotions come allow them to flow without becoming lost in them. New information will probably come as you recall the imagery.

✿ Frequently a very powerful image occurs which will become a model that you can retain and use to quickly move into this enlightened space.

✿ If a person appears, he will have a spiritual demeanor with a pleasant appearance which you can recall at later times. When you request to see this figure he/she will return. Use him as a guide or as a stepping stone onward.

✿ When your person appears be particularly aware of the physical setting and structures that you can recall in his spiritual space.

# INSTRUCTIONS

## BUILDING A TEMPLE

❖ You know your lighted path well by now. Start your walk toward the lighted heavens. The entire world takes on a luminescent glow. You are going to find a spot to build your temple. When you start you do not know its location. But you do know that with spiritual intent, you will erect a real and substantial structure to bridge the material and mystical worlds.

❖ Notice what you see as you move into grand vistas. Eventually one location will attract you for its purity and personal meaning. This can be on a mountain top, a bold rocky outcropping, a broad valley or desert, a forest or by water. Don't intellectually decide.

❖ When the location becomes clear and you are thrilled that you have found it, sit quietly to image the shape and substance of the temple structure you will build for yourself. You will determine its shape and size by your deepest needs for a place to encourage your spiritual thoughts. Pause long enough to turn on the "Elevating Tape" from the *Music of Light* tape set.

❖ Now build your structure. Be deeply involved and excited as it takes shape. If you don't like one part, change it. You have infinite opportunities. Don't be in a hurry. Great structures take time to construct and to experience.

❖ When your temple is complete, put in an entrance way and a door to enter. Landscape or leave it natural as you wish. Now erect a plaque or a logo to announce that this is your house of worship. Make it as simple or as elaborate as the structure suggests.

*88*

❖ Now enter your temple to complete the inside. Sit for awhile to experience the essence, the vibrations and let these tell you how to decorate, the colors, the substances and the objects you will put into it. Decorate one section as your private niche or alter, where you can sit to comprehend your God.

❖ Now that your physically creative work is over, sit quietly and meditate. Take possession of your temple.

❖ Let the light which was your guiding beacon at the beginning of this trip irradiate and engulf your church or temple in quiet beauty. You are content that this structure is correct for you.

From this divine space know that you are safe and loved. Allow yourself to follow the imagery which follows. As your meditation naturally terminates feel your radiance. Be not concerned with what you will do with it. Be only aware that this radiance will lead you.

❖ Slowly from this inner mystical place you will move in consciousness outward to the material world taking the divine light and the essence of God with you. It is yours wherever you go.

❖ Remember that you have soundly created your temple. During the time it took to build and decorate it, its imagery became carved into your mind-field.

# ❦ SUGGESTIONS ❦

✿   After each session spend some time recalling the details of your experience. Remember this locks memory firmly in your brain for instant recall.

✿   It is possible to have rapid insight into the profoundness of the experience you may have had.  But each time you return to your mystical creation it becomes more firmly imbedded in your consciousness.

✿   It is even better if you do not follow these instructions too carefully so that your own imagination better guides your imagery and experiences.

✿   Remember that the structure you created manifests where you are now.  If you built from your highest expectations it will stand as a symbol of you for a long time. However, if you built a lesser structure which you know deeply is temporary, fleeting images may occur of another grander temple you will eventually build from your highest self.

# ❧ INSTRUCTIONS ☙
## DEDICATING THE TEMPLE

*W*hen you are prepared to dedicate your temple in a group ceremony you are empowered to manifest your spiritual consciousness to the world.

✦ Take pride in your invitation list. Yes, choose persons whom you love who will also give you comfort in a new role. But choose from those persons in history whom you and civilizations have admired. Be not humble because by your creation and dedication you have joined the greatness of humanity. If you ask them they will come.

✦ Decorate appropriately for your ceremony and plan your service. This is your show, the music, the light and the thoughts.

✦ Give your dedication words with strength and radiance. You are sharing a real structure you have built. You are announcing to the world that you have found and taken back a divine power which you allowed to slip from you many years, centuries and lifehoods ago. And you are demonstrating to your loved ones that your power is a God-given capacity that is available to all humans.

✦ When the ceremony is over, its essence has permeated each soul and the greats and friends have gone about their lives. Give deep thanks for the divine energy which has assisted you in experiencing the greatness that all humans can reach.

# ❦ SUMMARY & CONCLUSIONS ❦

$\mathcal{N}$ote that throughout these meditations your consciousness has progressed from the grounding reality of walking in a stream, to anchoring your vibrations in earth and biology, to moving into and through some of your emotional barriers by following the light. You expanded your consciousness into divine vibrations which you anchored in a real material structure to house your expanding spirituality.

As you now know all spiritual experiences are mystical. They are not the primary reality of the material world, but they are equally as real. The energy that we associate with God and the expression of "I am" has changed to "I am" in divine vibrations which I experience and know to be the ultimate reality.

You may notice that now your prayers change from asking God to do something for you and to change situations, to asking for the strength and insight to move my own and the consciousness of mankind to assist this planet in its evolution.

Remember divine work is done by humans who have accepted the power, the responsibility and the humility to co-create with God. Then we will have grown from the concept that we are God's children to be worthy of being called God's co-creators.

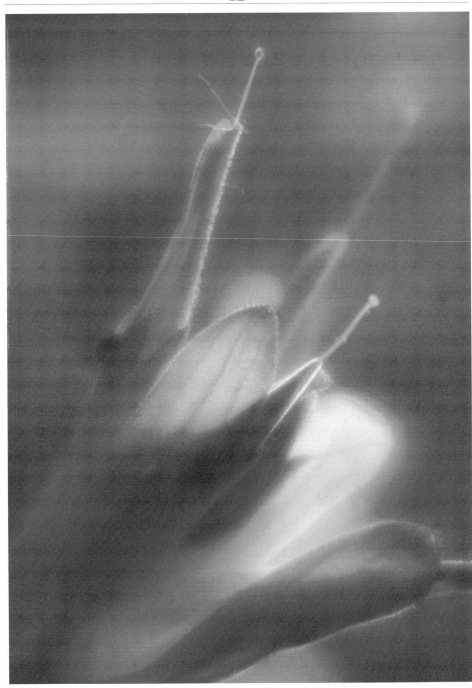

92

# Chapter 7

# TRANSFERRING THOUGHT

$T$he first six chapters of Mind Mastery Meditations focused your attention inward to perfect the strength, flow, and range of your human energy field. Then your goal was to access and to integrate all levels of human consciousness simultaneously so that life decisions could stem from a wealth of information from the body, the intellect and the soul. These all cohered into vast wisdoms to guide your behaviors, your life choices and even our civilization. With the Mind Mastery capabilities that you have gained from prior exercises you will be able to reach out to manifest your subtle consciousness skills with other people through silent transfer of thought.

This chapter on telepathic knowing and the transfer of thought speaks about information crossing great distances by uncommon methods. Ordinary information from remote places comes to us through the sense endings of our eyes, ears and nose, all distance receptors. These senses are effective for obtaining information within our sight focus and our hearing range or downwind from a scent. But these senses are limited to local information about material happenings as perceived by ordinary awareness. In this chapter, however, we are concerned with non-material space and happenings on a finer, more basic level --- the level of the field, where the interconnectedness of the entire universe occurs; where all fields of information flow back and forth sustaining and changing each field; where emotions take place and where evolutionary processes occur.

This part of the universe not experienced by ordinary senses, we frequently miss because our mind-field, its perfect receptor, is weak and relatively inactive. Even if we receive signals from far away we may disregard the information because we don't understand field phenomena. We have not learned that our mind-field is a powerful broadcasting and decoding system like radio and television. We can transmit information great distances by waves from sending to receiving antennae to be changed into sounds and images. Furthermore, our minds can send information as fast or faster than any manmade communication system and they can more accurately pinpoint the target. Before communication takes place there are thoughts. Thoughts however, are like quicksilver; they are on the move, peripatetic and elusive once they have been thought. Have you ever kept a notepad beside your bed or wished you had, to jot down thoughts and dreams that slip away as fast as you create them.

We have even hypothesized that the highest function of the mind resides in the field not in the senses, which makes it privy to all information. There are, however, some glitches in our recording system, the interface between mind and brain, where momentary mind thoughts are lost. And furthermore, even if the information is stored, often we cannot activate our brain recorder to remember it.

# INSTRUCTIONS

## PREPARING MIND AND BRAIN

Since both the mind and the brain are involved with telepathy and thought transfer, here is a meditation to normalize the energy and action by tuning both brain hemispheres. This can be done sitting or lying with your eyes closed.

✧ Practice the breathing meditations to expand the energy field's flow by breathing through the chakras upward from the feet to the head. Spin the chakras clockwise using color in your imagery (Chapter 2 - Activating the Physical).

✧ See a white ping-pong ball held above your right ear. Imagine that you gently shoot that ball over to the left ear through your brain. Then shoot it back to the right ear.

✧ Do this as many times as you need to until it takes no effort. The ping-pong ball should zip smoothly across from one hemisphere to the other, back and forth.

94

❀  This is a good exercise to equalize energy in the hemispheres when one hemisphere has been overactive with rational thought or the other has dominated with creative imagination.

❀  Frequently headaches will calm down.

❀  Persons with dyslexia are generally helped by this meditation.

❀  Frequently the movement of the ping pong ball is faster going in one direction. This indicates that you are overusing one hemisphere at that time.  Do this exercise more often when this occurs until the speed of the ball in both directions becomes equal.

❀  If you have been driving distances on an open road and come to a city with congestion, do this exercise the first time you stop at a light.  Your brain will become more alert to signals, signs and other autos afterwards.

95

# ❦❦INSTRUCTIONS❦❦

## MIND THOUGHT - BRAIN RETRIEVAL

*T*he next meditations should improve your skills in being aware of your mind's stream of events the interfacing of mind and brain and improved brain recall.

✢ Ground your field, either by the rope tied from around your waist to the boulder, or by bringing energy up through your left foot on inspiration, across your lower back and down through your right leg on expiration.

✢ Spin your chakras clockwise: red, the root chakra; orange, the kundalini; yellow, the emotional body; green, the heart; blue, the throat; orchid, the third eye; and white, the crown.

✢ Think of some creative project you have not done for lack of time or not knowing how to tackle it. Perhaps it is a repair job, reorganizing an office or room, or going shopping with no specific purpose in mind.

✢ Pick something that spontaneously comes to you. Watch your imagery as you are aware of your thoughts. With your imagination carry out the project.

✢ Have the intent before you start to record all thoughts in your brain for retrieval.

✢ Open your eyes and remember the details of your project. Tell a friend or an imaginary interested person or just speak them out loud.

# ❦ SUGGESTIONS ❧

✿ You can practice recall whenever you are aware of daydreaming and you do not immediately actively express your thoughts out loud.

✿ If you vividly remember your thoughts you may not need to repeat this Mind Mastery Meditation.

# INSTRUCTIONS

## TELEPATHY

*Y*ou have ample personal justification of your telepathic capacity when your awareness is focused. You think of someone and she calls. Something happens which you had already known or you experience others' feelings from a distance. Transfer of thought implies that something going on in one mind-field is traversing space, being intercepted and decoded by another. Conversely, it means that your mind-field is also in touch with many fields, all carrying information. If you record, organize and decipher this information, you know something without apparent sources.

### Think of a friend

✤ During a rest break, before bedtime or at the beginning of a regular meditation think of a friend. Allow your imagery to traverse space and see what that friend is doing. Don't struggle just allow the imagery to flow. You may see him in everyday or unusual activities.

✤ Continue your observation as though you were there with your friend. Communicate with him by projecting thoughts that spontaneously come to you.

✤ Before your imagery leaves him, ask him to call you. When he does, find out if he was aware that you were intentionally communicating telepathically with him. And ask if he was aware of an impulse to call you.

98 ✤ You share where you saw him and what he was doing. Regardless of your accuracy, your skills in telepathy will improve if you believe that they will as you practice.

# SUGGESTIONS

✿ This is an area of thought where many fear to tread. Even if you recognize this skill in others you may not see it in yourself --- you may still harbor some resistance to this skill.

✿ Know that this is the beginning of an elaborate yet normal personal skill in which your own mind-field computer can access all information if you punch in the proper code. The code is that you ask your higher mind to answer a defined question that you expect to be answered. If you don't get the answer at first try again, this time with insistence.

✿ You must seal your "code" question with strong intent and a clear, sure realization that your mind will do the work.

✿ Don't be surprised if the information requested comes to you without conscious thought or if a person calls you to provide the information. The caller may not even know why he called until you two spoke.

✿ Even with field concept explanations this process is difficult to comprehend because of its awesome reality --- the reality that you have access to the "Akashic Records" of all important thoughts and events in the universe. But during profoundly creative times in each of our lives we all discover this telepathic level of our minds.

# ❦❧ INSTRUCTIONS ❦❧

## TELEPATHIC SENDING AND RECEIVING

This series of meditations provides direct experiences to telepathically send and receive messages by thought. Their goal is not to transfer complex information but to sharpen your capacity to send and receive simple messages where the quality of thought experienced without words or gestures is more important than the idea. You should know whether thoughts are clear and articulate or poorly formulated and muddled, just as you do with the spoken word.

For direct feedback you need a partner. You can sense emotional tenderness or harshness when the senders' thoughts are emotionally charged. Those private little thoughts we keep to ourselves are available to others, particularly if these become emotionally charged when we attempt to hide them.

We average people in ordinary situations do not grasp details from others' thoughts but information is available to communicate something. And of course until we become more skillful we will limit our accuracy because we will interpret what we sense along with our predetermined biases and interests.

### Sender

✤ For this exercise you will need a partner.

✤ Facing your partner, sit closely but not touching. Decide which will be the sender and which the receiver on the first exercise. The role will reverse.

✤ Because you both will be sending and receiving information from your mind-field, you must be able to concentrate thought in the field. This is different but not difficult.

✤ Visualize putting thought in your field around your body not concentrated in your head. You will be activating your sixth sense, not your ordinary ones.

✤ Senders practice by turning "on" in your field; then think "off". Repeat that until you are aware that you are projecting thought through your field.

✤ Just project thought clearly with the intent that it can be decoded. Don't try to push it into a person.

### Receiver

✤ Receiver, put your antenna out and around you. Experience your mind in your field. You are to passively sense the information in the sender's field.

✤ Do your breathing exercises to expand your field. Allow it to meet the sender's field and to blend with it.

✤ Upon inhaling you will concentrate on the sender's field with all the information contained there.

✤ Let your mind-field gain impressions of what information the sender is broadcasting. Do not consciously try to figure out what the sender is sending; if you do you will totally block the sixth sense. Other senses will never get a clue.

✤ Alternate sender and receiver with the above instructions.

# Communicate Names

## Sender

✤ Ask the name of your receiver if this is a group session. Remember that person's name. Think of five or six common names of persons of the same sex. Include the name or nickname of your receiver in the group of names.

✤ Now out loud, say to your receiver "*Your name is:* _____ ." The sender is now quiet; he does not speak but projects one of the names into his field.

## Receiver

✤ You have heard the sender say "*Your name is* _____ " followed by his thought of a name; you intuitively respond immediately. If you experienced that the sender thought your name, say yes. If you experienced that the sender thought another name say no.

✤ Sender, repeat the names in a different series by always preceding your thoughts of a name with "*Your name is* _____." Remember the names where the receiver responded correctly.

✤ Alternate sender and receiver with the same instruction.

# ❧ SUGGESTIONS ☙

❀ Clues at the beginning may seem so nebulous that you are unsure. Be intuitive. This is the highest integrated level of knowing.

❀ Take the attitude that you are learning a skill not testing yourself, so you have no judgment about what you perceive.

❀ The best receivers don't strain to get information. They just go into neutral, focusing only on the partner's field. They let the impressions come to them.

❀ Some people are better senders that receivers. Others easily understand another's thoughts. With numerous partners you can understand your capabilities.

❀ Remember, your lack of success as a sender may be that you are trying to thrust the names at the other person rather than simply placing them in your field to be intuitively decoded by them.

❀ Sender, share with the receiver the accuracy of their answers and any name other than their own which he accepted. (Once when working with a group of Catholic priests I had the senders interject the name of Jesus Christ. Interestingly, some priests constantly accepted Jesus Christ as their own name.)

# INSTRUCTIONS

## COMMUNICATE A GREETING

✤ Sender and receiver select several one word greetings or short phrases such as: hello, good morning, nice to see you, or how are you?

✤ Both sender and receiver put your minds in your fields. The receiver is focused on input interpretation; the sender is on output projection.

✤ The sender states: *I greet you with_____?* (He thinks one of the greetings decided upon). The receiver intuitively answers which greeting the sender used. Your quick answers will be more accurate.

✤ Sender, repeat several times to see if particular words carry over better in thought with your receiver.

✤ Exchange sender and receiver roles.

102

# ❦ SUGGESTIONS ❦

❀ The accuracy of the communication is relative to the skill of both sender and receiver. You may be a better sender than receiver or vice versa. With some senders you may clearly get the answers. With others you flounder without information.

❀ Remember we are interested only in impressions of the thought communicated not specifically the details. At first, until you can clearly have control over your mind and brain, you may not be able to differentiate the thoughts of another person from your own.

# ☙INSTRUCTIONS❧

## COMMUNICATE FEELINGS

✤ Sender, think of a very happy emotional experience you have had. Put your happiness out in your mind-field all around you.

✤ Receiver, allow your conscious mind-field to give you an impression about whether the sender's thoughts were pleasant or unpleasant.

✤ Receiver, when you have an impression tell the sender.

✤ Sender, continue with the memory of positive and/or negative experiences which you broadcast from your field. Verbally tell your receiver when you are thinking about a different experience.

✤ Receiver, interpret when you have an intuitive impression.

✤ Exchange sender and receiver roles.

## COMMUNICATE COLORS OR FOODS

✤ Sender, using the same procedure try the following thought cues: i.e., "*Do you like_____?*" (Potatoes, beef or carrots, etc.) Sender, "*Do you like the color _____?*" (blue, yellow or violet).

✤ Sender, speaks "*Do you like the color_____?*" (think a pure color: red, orange, yellow, green, blue, violet or white).

104 ✤ Receiver, as soon as you have an impression about what food and color was projected by thought, respond with "*No, I don't like*" or "*Yes, I do like.*"

✤ Receiver, when you have an impression of color tell the sender. Perhaps you will know the color communicated by thought.

✤ Exchange sender and receiver roles.

# ❧ SUGGESTIONS ❧

✿ Sender, use only primary and secondary colors, not blends and project only one at a time.

✿ Use only single foods not casseroles or mixed foods like salads.

✿ Sender, you recall as many pure foods as you can but only one at a time.

✿ Sender, note the kinds of foods most accurate, ie: meats, vegetables, sweets, and the colors consistently predicted.

✿ Receiver, note the patterns of your accuracies and errors.

## CREATIVITY

Creativity describes the manipulation of information in new ways. It comes from a process of simultaneously recovering information stored in the brain (the result of prior field experiences) and in the mind-field and integrating this information with new experiences the mind is having. Creativity, the magical synthesis, is truly the highest level of thought.

Reflexive work such as walking, gardening and driving or the change in ordinary reality experienced during daydreaming set the stage for creativity. With aging creativity often dwindles. Our rootedness in habitual reality doesn't allow freedom for creative thought and problem solving but some older people sustain vibrational flexibility and with more stored information grow in creativity. They have learned to disregard or displace cultural and habitual restrictions in consciousness. Remember that higher consciousness holds emotional energies which we tend to block, thus stifling our creative processes.

Creativity comes from successfully blending the material and intuitive realities. Aldous Huxley equated creativity with deep reflection, with profound psychological withdrawal from awareness without losing physical realities. This requires intense focus during which everything not pertinent is set aside for the complete metaphysical absorption in matters of interest to the person. In deep reflection a person can summon up stored memories while also new information, juxtaposing both to create original thought. Highly creative people have illuminating flashes of insight when mind and brain blending occur.

**106**

## SELF THOUGHT - MANIPULATING OBJECTS

The next experiences expand your creative skills by bringing together two levels of information processing.

❖ Prepare by checking the flow of your field and establishing a relaxed physical state. Energize your brain hemispheres with the ping-pong game.

❖ Close your eyes; expand your mind-field; wipe your television screen clean and go into neutral thought. Await the first object to appear. Just let it project on your screen --- don't try to remember an object.

❖ Concentrate your focus on that image until it spontaneously changes to another object. You may have an ah-ha image that you did not expect.

❖ Observe the new object until it changes again. This provides a flow and gives flexibility to your attention.

❖ Stop imagining more objects. Select one object already imaged to work with.

❖ Next encourage your imagination to see all the possible things you could do with that object; make something new out of the object or image different functions for the object. Enjoy strange combinations that occur as you progress beyond practical uses. Allow yourself the freedom to create things that don't make logical sense and even border on the impossible.

# ❦ SUGGESTIONS ❦

✿ If you are in a group or with a friend share your creative thoughts.

✿ Was this easy for you and did you enjoy it? Or did it take some time to get the hang of such a sensitive exercise? Did it relax you or create tension?

✿ The purpose of this meditation was to join two levels of awareness, two streams of consciousness in a creative way. Too often we operate on only one at a time, mitigating expansive thoughts.

# INSTRUCTIONS

## PROBLEM SOLVING

✢  Wipe your television screen clean and prepare your field and physical body for higher consciousness thought.

✢  Ask yourself, for what problem would I like more alternative solutions?  Let the problem come to you.

✢  Pose a question or problem.  Using the same content ideas rephrase the question until you get a succinct statement.  Now ask or even re-ask that question of your higher consciousness.

✢  Don't choose emotionally-charged life and death problems for your first creative problem solving.  The problem can be either personal or impersonal in nature.

✢  Eliminate solutions that you have already thought about.  Probably these have been rationally overworked.  You want fresh ideas even if your logical brain calls these impossible.

✢  Allow yourself numerous solutions with detail to come to your imagery.  Record these in brain memory.

✢  Now evaluate your new answer to discover if you have created some better solutions or if you have created some new dimensions to the problem beyond what you consciously thought.  Remember the old adage "you cannot solve a problem on the level that you think created the problem".

# ❦ SUGGESTIONS ❦

❀   Throughout these Mind Mastery Meditations I have encouraged you to ask questions on one level of reality and await the answer from another level.

❀   The ability to choose a significant problem or to phrase the important question will determine the success and the level of your creative answers. Asking the right questions is more important to problem solving than the answers that you receive. If the question is clear the answers will come immediately and be understandable.

❀   Don't interpret your first imagery. This will bring creative closure. Even if these new answers are good on one level, they may not be on a deeper level.

❀   Over time the best solutions will stick if you trust and surrender.

# INSTRUCTIONS

## LATERAL THINKING

$\mathcal{A}$s you learn to elaborate thoughts more and more by lateral thinking you gain skills in the process. Some meditation exercises follow.

❖ Consciously force yourself to think with new classifications.

❖ Look around the room or place where you are. See the objects filling the space. Instead of lumping these into familiar categories such as tables, rugs, etc., make up new unfamiliar groups, like a round, square, or color classification. Use the objects in an unorthodox way or transform this place using all the objects for an unusual function.

❖ When you have finished be aware of what happened without apparent effort. Tell a friend or speak out loud to yourself, remembering your lateral thoughts. They often get richer with each remembrance.

❖ Think of a place you would like to go on a vacation. Eliminate all pre existing locations. Create one which may not exist in reality but which would have everything that you desire for your perfect vacation. Who is with you? What is the terrain like? Where do you live? And what do you do? What and where would you eat? And sleep? Who would you meet?

110

# ❦ SUMMARY AND CONCLUSIONS ❦

*T*his chapter introduced progressive exercises to gain skill in transferring thought and telepathic knowing. The first exercise prepared the brain and mind by repeating meditations from Chapter 2 to activate the field and relax the physical body. These were followed by a new exercise to balance the brain hemispheres, the ping-pong exercise. The second series was designed to develop skill in tapping into telepathic senses and recording these memories in the brain. The third group of meditations was for integrating mind and brain simultaneously, where the brain remembered simultaneously with the mind continuing to experience new thoughts. The last series of meditations was for gaining skill by using all the above skills in lateral extended thinking and in creativity. You have had sequential experiences to expand linear logical handling of information while integrating the creative intuitive method so that these blend without separation.

You were given opportunities to integrate your consciousness by posing clearly stated linear questions to the intuitive part of your consciousness. By learning to await answers from a higher source you have confirmed the integration of your consciousness. The creative meditations were so broadly directed that the goals did not overshadow the creative experience. Your "will" can direct your life choices with greater wisdom when mind and brain fully cooperate on all levels of awareness. From these Mind Mastery Meditations you should have learned that the freedom of creativity and the depth of wisdom are more important measures of your evolution than how high your awareness soars.

*111*

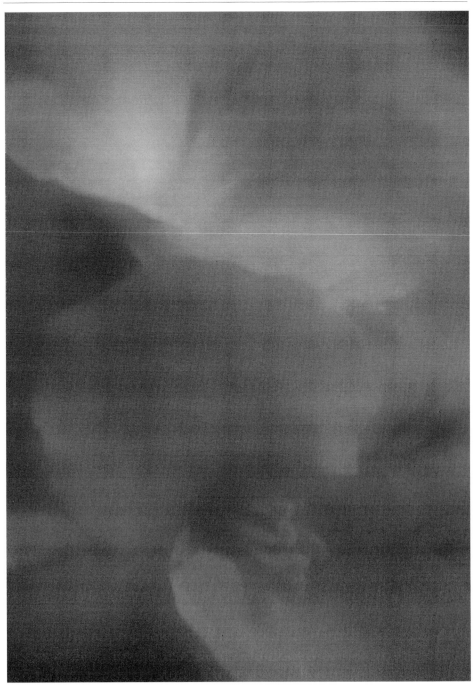

# Chapter 8
# ❧ℭ Sensing The Biocosmic Confluence ℭ❧

*T*his chapter will show you how to focus on the earth's electromagnetic milieu which supports us and the dynamic vibrations which activate us from near and far. You will learn to expand your awareness still further to sense the constant communication between your biological field and the fields of the universe. You will begin to understand how your electromagnetic transactions change both you and the cosmos. You will experience the interactions and transactions which sustain your body, mind and consciousness being fed by the powerful electromagnetic energy of earth and sky. This is the electrical energy which flames life. We are all acquainted with our human needs for oxygen, water and food. We know that the universe provides this. But most of us fail to comprehend that basic to all chemical actions lie electrical charges which trip off life and keep it going.

In this chapter you will learn to access the universal repository of vibrating energy for your physical vigor, your emotional strength, your intellectual potency and your spiritual power. The goal is to live more abundantly each day. Just as when we surround ourselves with the richness of art and music with a heightened awareness we can process more natural energy, enliven our sixth sense and enrich our years. This expansion will enable you to feel your infinite being and your belongingness, to experience your oneness with the universe.

## EARTH

*T*he structure of the earth that physically grounds us to its surface, and consciously to material reality, is powerfully alive with lower spectrum electromagnetism. Actually, all atoms including the atoms of the human body, wherever they exist in the universe are the same. And yet how these atoms are structured as molecules of the body or as molecules of soil, for example reveals a broad choreographic range of vibrations. The more densely the atoms are packed, the lower the frequency. For example, volcanic earth carries the red vibrations of the cooled molten lava; it is our most potent grounding force; it hyperactivates our tissues and systems. Because of its crystalline nature sand created by tumbled rocks and shells has the highest frequencies but it is not the richest of the ground surfaces. Fine grained alluvial soil is the most abundant type of earth substance and when moist is the most highly electrically charged. It supports profuse vegetation. When water is available the finely pulverized soil minerals go into solution creating an electrolytic, highly charged electrical condition. You have probably experienced the vitality of sitting unencumbered on the earth or sleeping on the ground. The native peoples tapped these electrical sources for vitality and healing. On the other hand rocky surfaces serve as a powerful transformer between earth and sky. To sit on rocks during rain or thunderstorm exponentially heightens the charges.

Also there are "hot spots" in the world where people gravitate to experience powerfully transcendent states of consciousness. Locations with radioactive minerals have been cherished as sacred healing sites. Possibly these "hot spots" correspond to the earth ley-lines. Certainly they are the chosen sites of man made stone structures such as the pyramids and Stonehenge. Some of these sites such as Delphi and

Medgegori, occurred naturally as places that stimulated societies to discover universal truths. These "hot spots" generally contain rocky formations, canyons, mountains; often they exhibit wind patterns between coastal and high desert areas. If you visit such a spot sit quietly on the ground, breathe through your entire field and sense the fundamental vibrations. Try the same exercise on the banks of the sea or a lake where the sands are damp from underground water. Each different composition and constellation offers a different colorful experience. All are biological stimulants which by nourishing the bodily tissue also create a tranquil effect. These earth vibrations provide coherent vitality that you will feel long after the outing.

## WATER

Living bodies of water also support the life of plants and animals with their magnetic charges. Minerals dissolved in water create an electrolytic ionized water. A tumbling stream with eddies, cascades and waterfalls powerfully breaks water into negatively charged ionized molecules which are essential to cellular activity. You have seen this phenomenon manifest in the lush plant growth around waterfalls.

Pounding waves against a rocky shore bring sea birds to nest in impossible crevices where energy vigorously nourishes their offspring. The sea life of crustacea and algae is multiplied by the energy released from the crashing waves. People gravitate to these rocky areas as they did to Northern Ireland where the land grew little but the vibrations nourished many. Seashore plants and flowers clinging to rocky cracks almost devoid of soil grow profusely. Energy is released from water in motion.

Mists, fog and rains are molecularly structured moisture with subtle electromagnetic effects. Have you ever wondered why car engines run so smoothly during rain and mist? After strong rain the birds sing louder. It's too bad that more of us don't protect ourselves from the cold and go for a long quiet walk in the rain to sense the heavily charged electrical energy. When we walk in the fog or mist, we smoothly expand our energy field. We will return more rested. When we swim or play in water we splash spontaneously without recognizing that moving water is more charged than stationary water. Likewise, showers refresh our electromagnetic field more than baths.

## LIVING ORGANISMS

Most of us like to live surrounded in our homes with living plants, flowers, bushes and trees. We set aside protected areas for native growth to bring beauty and to enrich our electromagnetic pools. Have you ever stopped, sat or hesitated in an area of lush growth and tuned into the vibratory differences of shrubs? Some plants are light with lacy leaves and a soft spiral growth pattern like ferns or climbers. These structure the atmospheric energy smoothly. Others with denser leaves and heavier stalks offer a rich, stabilizing, substantive block of energy, like the crepe myrtle or camellia. If you live near the desert or have in your home small succulent plants, place your hand over these plants and breathe through your field into your hand. Without looking your sixth sense will help you describe perfectly their shapes and their gray, green soft color. When you select indoor plants be sure to broaden your electromagnetic diet with a variety of sizes, shapes and types of plants. People coming into your home will sense its aliveness.

Your reaction and transaction with natural vegetation nourishes your electrical field.

Take a few moments in your busy schedule to sense growing vegetation.  Do it purposely and with specific focus to transact with their unique vibrations.  Find trees to stand or sit under and to lean against.  When you tune in you will sense the nature of the root system, whether it spreads broadly or penetrates deeply with a tap root.  Move your consciousness up to the trunk to sense how the atmospheric energy is altered based on the shape of the trunk and limbs and the density of its bark and wood.  Move your awareness out to the branches and leaves.  Note that some trees spread energy out into space or like a palm tree turn energy back down upon you and the land.  When standing beside cypress or poplar trees you will feel the energy shoot upward toward the heavens.  Sample many trees in different environs.  Experience their energy not just their appearances.  Some tree vibrations you will like better than others.

## ANIMALS

We have had no way other than intuition to evaluate the electromagnetic energies provided our planet by living creatures.  Astrophysicists have discovered a belt of radiation circulating the globe about 50 miles deep with strong 500 cycles per second energy, a red vibration.  They have been unable to locate the source.  Satellite sampling of other planets does not show this red cycle belt.  It is interesting that the base biological fields of warm blooded animals peak at 500 cycles per second.  This leads us to speculate that the vibration from biological tissue constantly produced by the many animals on earth may hover in a belt around this planet.  Regardless of the source, this 500 cycle belt is available to stimulate life on earth if we choose to transact with it.

115

There is considerable evidence that older persons who have domesticated animals are nourished by their affection and loyalty.  My research shows that when animals are held and petted and spoken to with affection a powerful transaction occurs between the two fields.  Both fields increase in strength and glow with radiant frequencies.  When affectionate dogs and cats are brought into convalescent hospitals and nursing homes recovery is hastened.  Persons who breed and raise animals comment about the increased supply of energy they sense.

The next time you are in a zoo you may gravitate to the aviary where many birds are grouped together in a small enclosure.  Sense the air that they move in their flight and the constant tonal variations of their songs.  These tones are in the upper ranges of the electromagnetic scale, as high as you can hear with your ears.  Your field will sense the unheard higher vibrations.  The multiplicity of the sounds of birds particularly when they are in groups provides us with gentle coherent energy in a wide frequency spectrum essential for expanded consciousness.

## ATMOSPHERE - STRATOSPHERE - IONOSPHERE

Air is always charged.  We have seen that air blended with water in the form of fog or mist amplifies electricity.  Now let us look at air  in motion, where movement of atoms against atoms also hypes up electrical charges.  Moderate temperature winds are about neutral in ionization but winds with Arctic cold and hot winds from high deserts to lower lands both release charged particles that effect us differently.  A cold wind, like a wet one, frees negative ions which increase the size of our auras and cause us to feel invigorated.  The hot winds release  positive ions which diminish the auric field and produce all manner of unpleasant physical and emotional symptoms. The unpleasant effects can be offset by restoring negative ions with a cool shower, a swim or immersing oneself in lush plant growth. But what is particularly stimulating is the sudden shift from positive to negative ions or vice versa. This happens often where high deserts approximate oceans and the prevailing winds shift from one mass to the other.

Cyclones and tornadoes, vortices of energy with tremendous wind velocity, form when the electrical activity pocketed in clouds is directed downward by atmospheric pressure changes. Hurricanes are spawned in the tropics above yet near the ocean surface where changes in atmospheric pressures create swirling air. This circular motion picks up large quantities of water which is released in violent wind driven rain storms. Because the vortices of hurricanes cover more space they last longer but have less force than tornadoes. An eye develops in the middle of the storm where there is motionless air, normal in oxygen content but nearly devoid of electromagnetic activity. This neutral space causes a short circuiting in the human nervous system which can cause breathing difficulties and heart attacks. Doesn't it seem strange that the center of a hurricane which we would expect to be peacefully still with motionless air is actually stressful because it lacks life-giving electrical energy? People who live in hurricane areas and in tornado alley know well their sheer physical power and many sense the tremendous electrical energy released to the local air and soil as the storms pass on.

Lightning, a form of electrically charged activity which splits air molecules, and creates thunder (the sound of the mechanical closure of the space) is the most direct natural electrical discharge over relatively large areas. One does not have to be in a straight line with lightning to see its awesome power; it lights up a dark sky and sparks electrical transformers. You feel shock when you are near natural conductors of water and metal. After an electrically charged rain the air is hypercharged.

Have you been thrilled by the beauty of polar lights, the Aurora Borealis, with its awesome display of patterns and colors? We may think it occurs only at night for that is when we see it, but astronomists tell us that it occurs even more powerfully in daylight. It is good that people who live in the northern hemisphere have this special electrical energy during the winter months when their land is denied some of the light energy from the sun. Actually, the sun indirectly causes the aurora. When the solar winds arising from sun flares strike the earth's polar ice cap they create the aurora.

Despite the destruction to humans, animals and plant life, these atmospheric storms replenish the earth's dynamic energy. As long as life requires a living earth it, too, must be fed. It is through these dramatic and often violent activities that the earth evolves. How wonderful it is if we accept the potential dangers, protecting ourselves with sturdy hurricane and earthquake-sound buildings and tornado cellars, so that we can appreciate the associated values. Then we can relish the enormous life giving energy these storms provide for us and the world. We can enjoy the electrical excitement.

## COSMIC HAPPENINGS

During the past ten years our understanding of the cosmos has increased more than in many preceding centuries. We formerly believed that there was only our galaxy. Now we know that a thousand such galaxies exist, each with its own sun.

The universe is now known to be immeasurably richer, more varied and more violent than we had ever dreamed of, exhibiting wave length bands above and below that of visible light.

Early mystic astrologers claimed that the earth's energy was created by some form of electromagnetic and mechanical energy arising from the crust and interacting with solar and cosmic radiation. Today astrophysicists are swamped with new information from huge earth lenses and space craft recordings from outer space. They are making revolutionary discoveries about the cosmos. They have found that sun spots of electromagnetic energy organize into a solar wind with atomic electrons and protons streaming outward from the sun. Ionized gases are created from the magnetic field of this solar wind. They have discovered that the winds of space (both solar and interstellar) differ from the winds that sweep this earth. Terrestrial winds and gases are cool (rarely reaching 90 degrees Fahrenheit) and slow (always below the speed of sound). The sunspot radiations, however, are very hot with much higher frequencies than the solar radiation.

Early German astronauts puzzled over the brilliant flashing lights they saw over the Himalayan and Chilean Andes mountains. They pondered the ancient prophecy that the spiritual light of the Himalayas would shift to the Andes. Probably a more accurate explanation comes from NASA with confirmation that the Andes has the strongest concentration of natural magnetism in South America. Astronomers say that the lights of the magnetic earth energy can be seen from space. They believe that the dry clear atmosphere over the Andes provides the transparent window between the earth and the universe. It is understandable why many new highly-equipped observation laboratories have sprung up in the high Andes and that the number of retreat and meditation centers is growing in the area.

The cosmos is a universe of vibrating energy fields and resonances nourishing the earth. The intensity of the earth's electrical field is maintained by the worldwide thunderstorm currents and varies in phase with cosmic radiation. Planetary electrical storms never cease. The light of the sun is life's driving force while moon cycles constantly affect the functioning cycles of the earth's water, animals and plants. Astrologists' early understandings about planetary orbits and their magnetic effects upon earth's subtle happenings are gradually gaining scientific credibility.

More and more we are understanding the self-organizing nature of the universe. We are coming closer to the ancient Chinese philosophies and to John Muir's apt observation in *First Summer in the Sierras, 1947*. "When we try to pick out anything by itself we find it hitched to something else in the universe."

*I*n those geographic locations where there is a more stable quantity of energy and a greater flow, people and animals live more peaceful, unchallenged lives; their birth rates tend to be lower, their health is more languid and they are less creative. Those locations with the greatest regular electromagnetic contrast, without acute overstress, stimulate physical, emotional, and intellectual vigor.

So often we have accepted the philosophical statement "we are one with the universe" without seeking evidence. Actually, we are like the universe in many ways. The simplest form of matter whether it be air, water, soil or a living organism is composed of atoms and all these atoms are the same. But this fact is overshadowed by how we are different. The ways identical atoms are organized into molecules, cells and systems and the operational instruction these higher structures receive causes them to look, behave and experience differently. For example, rocks and soil with the same atoms differ based upon their source, be it volcano, tumbling water or underground pressure. The instructions in the seed of a plant always produce the same kind of plant be it fern or a giant tree. The genes in the seed of an animal always produce a duplicate animal in coat, color and programmed behavior. The even more complex genetic instruction of humans provide nervous systems, brains and mind. Remember, simple instruction makes for uncomplicated mechanical reactions with the universe. More complex organisms have both mechanical reactions and interactions with the universe's fields. The most complex organizations have the mechanical reactions, the field interactions, and because of the complexity of the nervous system, brain and mind they also selectively transact with complex fields. This means that man and higher animals can consciously modify their interaction and how they communicate with higher fields. By his communication man reorders himself and profoundly influences all living structures. Simply, we can turn up and turn down as well as twist around how we affect and are affected by outside atomic structures. We can reorder anticoherent fields and send coherent ones into chaos. We will gain health and grow in consciousness as we progressively gain mastery over the subtle energies of our world. Then our bodies and minds will be able to lead and follow in the dance of life with the great pools of energy of the natural environment.

Take time in your busy day to purposely experience and revel in your natural world all around you. You will be nourished if you focus your awareness on natural things, don't just leave it to happenstance. Plan to tune into the soil, the rocks, the sand on a vacation or at the beach or mountains, so that you can sense these basic energies. Weeding or trimming your garden is perfect if you experience these growing plants while you automatically weed. Make it a ritual of sensing not just a task to be completed.

How often do you stop to let your mind and senses play with a glowing sunset, to follow its colors irradiating the sky and land until it is gone? Do you ever languish in the essence of the full moon like native people who live there in their dream time? Have you ever thrown open your window to experience the awesome energy of distant lightning and felt your body quiver and emotions quicken as you reorder energy into your tissue? How often have you sought out or even hesitated when wild creatures appear, to send and receive messages from them? It is interesting that we are enthralled by nature programs without realizing that on a smaller scale we can have a real experience with living things. You water your house plants dutifully but

118

how often do you talk to them?  Place your hands near them and watch and feel them move in circles to your energy.  When you need refreshment do you stop at a park, at a waterfront, roll down your windows and drink in the natural essence?  If you rush home to  get to the gym, why not take a few evenings for a walk in nature?

Because we humans do not have nerve endings for directly sensing electro-magnetism, we will sense it in the form of color, shape, sound and the flow of air.  But all these impressions also feed our sixth sense, the sense of the immaterial.  You will interact with your world out of reflex and half-heartedly even if you do nothing but exist.  You will only improve your skill when you practice focusing your attention on the biocosmic connection.  When you do this your transactions will profoundly nourish your total being and you will find yourself on every level both separate yet one with God's phenomenal universe.

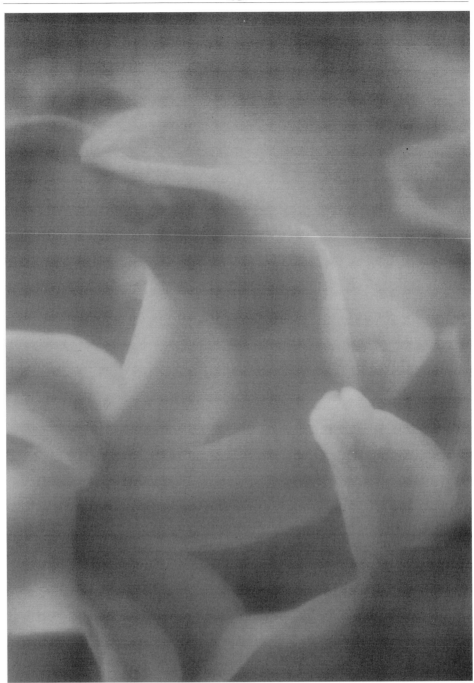

120

# *For Your Enjoyment*
# *Additional Discoveries*

By
Dr. Valerie V. Hunt

Enlightening Tapes Of Human Energy Fields

Music And Auric Sounds

Color Video With Auric Sounds And Pictures

Available From

MALIBU PUBLISHING CO.
P.O. Box 4234
Malibu, CA 90264

TEL (310) 457-4694
FAX (310) 457-2717

# MUSIC OF LIGHT: AURIC SOUNDS

*T*he world's first authentic sounds produced by the human auric field are harmonically correlated with contemporary, classical, and especially composed music. Designed to replenish and make coherent the human energy field. Listeners have described these tapes as a work of art... a magnificent experience associated with feelings of improved vitality and well-being.

**STABILIZING**
RAINBOW

Progressing in frequency, 13 rich, nourishing and coherent color sounds blend as white light to stabilize the field and encourage broad awareness.

**VITALIZING**
RED - AMBER - ORANGE

Vibrant stimulating sounds revitalize the physical body and activate spontaneous emotions.

**TUNING**
YELLOW - GREEN - GOLD

Fine tuning of sensation and perception improves nervous system efficiency and performance and creatively activates the mind.

**RELAXING**
BLUE - VIOLET- MAUVE

Soothing relaxing spectrum encourages a quiet contemplative state of peaceful higher consciousness.

**ELEVATING**
WHITE - BLUE - GOLD

Etheric spiritual tones elevate thoughts and imagery to a broader world, richer beauty and deeper wisdom.

**COST:** 5 Tapes, 60 Minutes Each, DOLBY Stero   (Not Sold Separately)
Includes Shipping & Handling $150.

# ❦ Video Tape ❦

## The Human Energy Field And Health

This video show, for the first time in color the dramatic sounds and pictures of the auric field and documented research slides of Dr. Hunt's amazing energy field findings during health, disease, pain, emotions, imagery and consciousness states.

**Cost:** Color VHS or PAL  -  60 Minutes
Includes Shipping & Handling $50.

# ❧ Lecture Tapes ❧

## International Healing Energy Medicine Conference
Regent's College, England, October 1992
Series by Dr. Valerie V. Hunt, Principal Lecturer

### BIOLOGICAL ENERGY FIELD AND ENERGY MEDICINE: INTUITIVE E DIAGNOSES

New concepts of the electromagnetic source of life and disease elucidates the current major medical problems: diabetes, sclerosis, fatigue syndrome, viruses, heart and Alzheimer's disease. All point to new diagnoses and treatment modes featuring close cooperation of physicians, psychics and healers.

### MIND: THE SOURCE OF PHYSICAL AND EMOTIONAL DISEASES

Major gaps in brain neurophysiology and an emphasis on chemistry with shots and pills to cure all health problems have treated symptoms with limited success and growing danger. Redirected basic research, however, discovers that the mind is a field of information, the true source of all health problems. Energy medicine is the visionary medicine of the future.

### FUTURE HEALING: ENERGY FIELD TRANSACTIONS AND CHANGE

124

Understanding the subtle energy systems that flow through body meridians, connective tissues and by neuropeptide transmission along with discovery of the elegant chaos pattern in the human field makes it understandable why a gentle energy nudge can snatch order out of the random chaos of extensive dysfunction and bring about miraculous healing and regeneration.

**COST:** 3 Lectures, 4 Tapes, 60 Minutes Each Tape
Includes Shipping & Handling $50.

## COLOR PREFERENCES, COLOR NEEDS, COLOR EFFECTS

Color preferences, effects and needs reflect our deepest responses to color. The color vibrations of our own "aura" constitute a color screen which alters and accentuates our visual color perception.

Objects do no possess a fixed color of their own: they only have changing vibrations which result in light reflections from the pigment these contain. It is the reflected light filtered through a person"s aura which favor his judgements to create his physical and emotional experience with color.

Electronic research is discussed as applied to the effects of color upon vitality and strength, relaxation, calmness, and extended sensory awareness.

**COST:** 90 Minute Tape, Includes Shipping & Handling $16.

## BIOCOSMIC CONNECTION

Research with brain waves, holograms and energy fields is broadly publicized in popular magazines so that many people embrace the philosophical beliefs of the oneness of man and the universe. But we have not known how these two separate material entities actually transact as one and the practical application of these transactions to our lives.

For the first time, pioneering research with high frequency electronics captured and elucidated the human energy field and observed field transactions; people with people, with atmosphere, with Earth vibrations, and with thought waves. From these studies a new model emerged of the macrocosmic links of humans and cosmos, and how the mind-field creates illness and health, underlies all communication and creativity and makes telepathy and clairvoyance rational.

**COST:** 90 Minute Tape, Includes Shipping & Handling $16.

125

# 🌷 *Book* 🌷

## Infinite Mind:
## Science Of Human Vibrations Of Consciousness
### BY VALERIE V. HUNT

❖ Living vibrations validated by electronic frequency research

❖ Higher mind discovery to be an energy field throughout the body

❖ New models of science and thought pinpoint human energy fields to be the source of all behavior

❖ Emotions as energy disclosed to be different at personality and soul levels of consciousness

❖ Healing and diagnosis of the frequency patterns of health and disease substantiate Alternative Medicine

❖ Mystical connections of higher consciousness found in creativity, healing and spirituality

❖ Spiritual connections discovered to occur when human vibrations are elevated and coherent

126

*"Years ahead of its time..."*
*"A classic you will read many times..."*
*"A monumental work for everyone's reading..."*

COST:  Includes Shipping & Handling                $33.50
                CA Residents Add Sales Tax $2.29        $35.79

---

## 🌷 *All Orders* 🌷

MALIBU PUBLISHING COMPANY

P.O. BOX 4234, MALIBU CA 90264
TEL (310) 457-4694
FAX (310) 457-2717

U.S. DOLLARS ONLY • MASTERCARD, VISA OR PERSONAL CHECKS